Bridge

Titles in the *Objekt* series explore a range of types – buildings, products, artefacts – that have captured the imagination of modernist designers, makers and theorists. The objects selected for the series are by no means all modern inventions, but they have in common the fact that they acquired a particular significance in the last 100 years.

Bridge

Peter Bishop

REAKTION BOOKS

For Luke.
There are still plenty of bridges to cross.

Published by Reaktion Books Ltd
33 Great Sutton Street
London EC1V 0DX, UK

www.reaktionbooks.co.uk

First published 2008

Printed and bound in China by Imago

British Library Cataloguing in Publication Data
Bishop, Peter, 1946–
    Bridge. – (Objekt)
    1. Bridges – Design and construction 2. Bridges
    I. Title
    725.9'8

    ISBN-13: 978 1 86189 346 8

Contents

Williamsburg Bridge, New York, completed 1903.

Introduction:
The Telling of the Bridge

Jazz on a bridge

A well-known story travels the jazz circuits. On a New York summer's evening in 1961 a music critic of *Metronome* magazine and his wife were strolling from Manhattan to their Brooklyn home, across the little-used pedestrian walkway on Williamsburg Bridge that spanned 488 metres (1,600 ft) over the East River. Directly in front they heard the sound of a saxophone in the hands of a gifted musician playing complex and sophisticated music. It was Sonny Rollins, already a legend, developing a piece of creative work as he struggled to emerge from a difficult and reclusive period. Between 1959 and 1961 Williamsburg Bridge, close to Rollins's home, was where he went to work on this new piece, aptly called *The Bridge*. Perhaps Rollins chose the site due to a single-minded insistence on prolonged place-immersion as part of his composition and performance, or maybe this was just a conducive spot. Rollins insisted that it was for privacy, both his and that of his neighbours, whom he did not want subjected to the loud noise of a saxophone at all hours. Perhaps it was the idea of the bridge that inspired him, a kind of creative cipher, one that condensed both physical structure and root metaphor of a collective imagining.

Certainly there was no shortage of representational contexts. The nineteenth-century bridges of New York had long been 'sung' and a plurality of narratives imaginatively told in a variety of mediums and genres, from poetry to cinema. The sheer physicality of these bridges was deeply integrated into the fabric of daily life in the city.[1] Some of these bridges had become integral characters in the various scripts of New York, not only as the unofficial capital of America, but the 'capital' of twentieth-century Capital, the pre-eminent global city. The widespread emergence of television, dominated by the US, and the post-war power of Hollywood ensured that, even by the late 1950s and early '60s the bridges of New York, particularly Brooklyn Bridge, were (along with San Francisco's Golden Gate) the most media-visible bridges in modern western popular culture. Williamsburg Bridge itself had featured prominently in the 1948 film *Naked City*, a crime thriller that culminated in a chase across the bridge.[2] But whatever the reasons for Sonny Rollins's choice of both practice site and theme for his composition, or the meanings generated by the various contexts in which we can place them, the story makes an appropriate starting point and offers a particular methodology for this exploration of the bridge.

While this is a multi-disciplinary study, a broadly communication and cultural studies perspective lies at its core. From within such perspectives, Jean Baudrillard usefully suggests three very different ways of organizing and studying objects. On the one hand there are formal systems of classification, which can be based around almost any criteria. For bridges these could be size, function, type of span, cost, date built, even type of failure, kind of risk involved, and so on. On the other hand, bridges, as with any object, could be studied as 'a kind of epic history of the technical object', a form of analysis which 'notes the changes in social structure associated with technological development'.[3] A third approach addresses such questions as 'how are objects experienced, what needs other than functional ones they answer, what mental structures are interwoven with – and contradict – their functional structures, or what cultural, infracultural or transcultural system underpins their directly experienced everydayness'.[4] Such an approach focuses on 'the processes whereby people relate to them and with the systems of human behaviour and relationships that result from them'.[5] In a general way, this study approaches the bridge from all three perspectives, with some jazz thrown in. It constantly attempts to contextualize bridges, not just to locate them within a particular setting but to understand them as key elements that actively shape their context. Attention must be given to the way in which a particular bridge is approached, not only conceptually or aesthetically, but also from a literal physical

New York Harbour and Brooklyn Bridge c. 1905.

standpoint. Brooklyn Bridge, for example, can be approached from the land or from the harbour. It can be placed in the foreground or in the background. Each approach reveals different contexts and meanings.

The modern bridge

While its ancestry is ancient, a certain kind of bridge and bridgeness emerged around 200 years ago as one of the prime monuments of modernity. Such a prestige was partly due to the sculptural qualities of bridges that were perfect for a conspicuous display of heroic engineering – for fantasies about overcoming nature, mastering new construction materials, displaying daring visions and computational certainties. It was a prestige that also owed much to a revolution in physical movement, on both a local and global scale, a revolution in mobility that was itself integral to modernity – the reliable and efficient circulation of goods, the

The Bridge. A night view of Brooklyn Bridge.

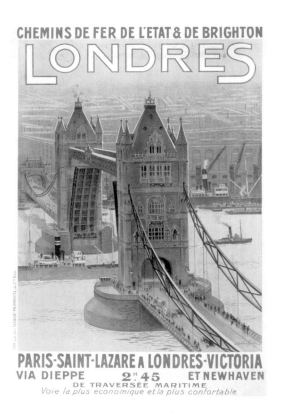

CHEMINS DE FER DE L'ÉTAT & DE BRIGHTON

LONDRES

PARIS·SAINT·LAZARE a LONDRES·VICTORIA
VIA DIEPPE   2ʰ·45   ET NEWHAVEN
DE TRAVERSÉE MARITIME
Voie la plus économique et la plus confortable

regulated and rapid mass movement of the population. Such a
revolution was also based around the new technologies of transportation and communication – the heroic age of railways in
particular, but also the rise of effective roads and of steamships.
This radical shift in the meaning, design, purpose and imagining
of bridges was simultaneously documented, celebrated and explored
through the visual and performing arts, through literary fictions,
through a documentary and news media that was radically transformed first by photography and then by cinema, through the
newly invented forms of visual reproduction such as postcards,

Londres, a 1930s poster for French railways.

posters and postage stamps. The modern bridge was also represented through an outpouring of new types of bridges and bridging projects, in new possibilities for physical bridges.

The twentieth century saw the golden age of the railway being supplanted first by that of the automobile and then of the aeroplane, forcing yet another re-evaluation of the bridge. New social ideologies and philosophies, new psychological and artistic paradigms emerged around and through the bridge. New paradigms of design and computation, new construction practices and new materials evolved within the shifting contexts of economics, planning and organization, patterns of everyday life and changing global relationships.

While at the dawn of the twenty-first century bridges still remain vital structures, physical transportation itself has been coupled with, and many of its functions supplanted by, vastly complex systems of digital electronic communications, of virtual travel and transportation. Cultural, imaginative, artistic, economic and political contexts have constantly changed during the history of the modern bridge, as have engineering design and practices, plus the development and creative utilization of new materials. There have been radical paradigm shifts as well in the scholarly disciplines that pay close attention to the bridge and to its contextualization.

This book examines the bridge (bridging and bridge-ness), along with the cultural practices – from the civic to the military, architectural to engineering, artistic, poetic and philosophical – that have circulated through it over the past two hundred years, from the onset of modernity to the dawn of the new millennium. The prime focus is therefore the fate of the bridge in western and other industrializing societies and cultures. The approach to such a broad question must of necessity be highly multifaceted, mobilizing a wide range of scholarly disciplines both as theoretical perspectives and as primary source material. In addition, numerous other sources are deployed, including paintings, written and visual fictions, written and visual documentaries, news, travel texts and advertising.

The bridge is an idea, a kind of imagining that has an ahistorical, archetypal sensibility and function. Bridge/bridging is a root metaphor of cultural and individual imagining. People from all walks of life and all ages dream bridges, engage in reverie on and around them, invent them, find meanings in them. However, this idea, this core fantasy, also shifts and changes from one historical culture to another. At the same time bridges are utterly historical and culturally specific. This applies to the manner of their design and construction, as well as their physical and imaginative use, whether at the time of construction and opening or much later – the subsequent use and symbolization of long existent structures. No less than its design, the representation of a bridge always embodies fantasy. Sometimes this imagining is cast in an apparently realist mode and sometimes one that more clearly shows its stylization and cultural origins.

Yoshitora Utagawa, *London and Pedestrian Bridges*, 1866, woodblock print triptych.

Telling the bridge: A double construction

Bridges are things about which stories are told. This telling is integral to the idea and practice of bridges. The varieties of ways such a telling has occurred, the mediums employed, the audiences, the historical shifts in the contexts of this telling, all need to be articulated and mapped. This book is one such telling. Ivo Andrić, in his classic 1946 novel *The Bridge Over the Drina*, tells how after the completion of a great medieval Ottoman stone bridge in Bosnia people 'began to remember details and to embroider the creation of a real, skilfully built and lasting bridge with fabulous tales which they well knew how to weave and to remember'.[6] In this sense two constructions are involved in the completion of a bridge, one of solid materials and the other of narratives. The multiple telling of the bridge involves shifting styles and contexts of representation. While most bridges are small, almost invisible, many have their own name, are the subject of stories, legends, tourist rhetoric and visual representation. Some bridges are famous and iconic. Others appear for just a moment on the historical stage – often due to war or accident.

The bridge, like other highly aestheticized objects such as art, food and fashion, is saturated with discourses, from those of the connoisseur to the dense technicalities of engineering and architectural design manuals. Individual bridges have been mobilized as benchmarks by which to measure the ranking of any particular civilization on a techno-architectural ladder of attainment. For example, there was widespread refusal in late nineteenth-century western Europe to accept the architectural and engineering capacity of the Ottoman Turks. As a result, architectural masterpieces like the main bridge at Mostar were wrongly attributed to the supposedly superior civilization of the Romans.[7] The capacity merely to

construct a bridge has been seen as a defining indicator of human civilization. The bridge is classed alongside tools and fire as a founding technology of human culture, for it enhances a necessary land-based mobility and connectivity. Bridges have also been seen as the expression of an individual's 'artistic brilliance', akin to sculpture and architecture, music and painting. As 'wonders of the world', bridges have been gathered in a variety of ways in order to stimulate pleasure, enjoyment and interest, as in the ubiquitous, and at times visually compelling, coffee-table books on the subject.

The intense visual presence of the bridge has long been celebrated by painting. But the invention of photography in the first half of the nineteenth century, an Industrial Revolution companion to the modern bridge, allowed its fuller exploitation. The aesthetics of the modern bridge became somehow intertwined with the new mode of photo-representation, as painting was freed from any lingering documentary obligation. Previously, given the restricted mobility of the general population in most societies, a bridge was

Golden Gate Bridge, San Francisco, 1984.

Mostar, Romer Bridge, Bosnia-Herzegovina, completed 1566, in the 1890s.

known directly only to those who lived in its locality; a famous bridge could only be known through oral narratives – gossip, rumour, travellers' tales. Cheap mechanical reproductive processes now allowed *the image* of the bridge, through countless numbers of photo reproductions, to achieve widespread circulation. The images of previously little-known bridges around the world, as well as more famous ones, were distributed through a diverse range of print media. New engraving processes and especially photography also allowed a fuller documentation of the bridge as a construction process. Through these technologies of visual mass reproduction bridges became inserted into a range of entirely new paradigms, desirable objects for the mass tourist gaze. The opening of a large bridge was, and remains, the occasion of spectacular display and ceremony, celebrations of national and civic pride. Throughout the nineteenth century bridges began to feature regularly on a range of commercial promotions. While cinema then continued this trajec-

Hell Gate Bridge, New York, under construction, 1915.

tory, it also provided yet another paradigm shift. In numerous films, from *Waterloo Bridge* to *Bridge on the River Kwai*, from *Les Amants du Pont-Neuf* (*Lovers on the Bridge*) to *Godzilla*, bridges have regularly featured, not just as pivotal dramatic settings, but as characters in themselves.[8]

But, while the compelling visual presence of the bridge has dominated imaginative engagement it has not completely effaced other approaches. Poetry, novels, myth and philosophy all have a long history of involvement with the bridge.[9] Andrić's novel *The Bridge over the Drina* is a story of sweeping historical proportions, about a medieval stone bridge in Bosnia, with eleven arches, 250 paces

The opening of the Brooklyn Bridge on the evening of 24 May 1883.

Empire Sewing Machine Co. New York, colour lithograph print, c. 1870, showing a completed Brooklyn Bridge, which was then under construction.

long and 10 paces wide. It is a central symbol of the establishment, duration and ending of a civilization, the Ottoman. The bridge connects epic events with an intensely local culture and everyday life. A vast historical complexity of religious, ethnic, cultural and geographic issues is condensed into the bridge. Initially constructed deep within the territory of an utterly secure Ottoman Empire with its internal communication and transportation requirements, the bridge carries the road to Sarajevo, linking Bosnia and Serbia. Then, as geo-politics changed in the late nineteenth century, the bridge was stranded beyond the Empire's extreme edge and unstable border. Its meanings and purpose altered dramatically as a result. In many ways this tale is a precursor to the tragedy that befell the bridge at Mostar at the very close of the twentieth century. Such fictional accounts, whether written and/or cinematic, allow a fulsome exploration of the gathering and dwelling-ness that permeates the bridge.

Hong Kong's Ting Kau Bridge (completed 1998) at night.

Rapid developments in sound recording have facilitated sophisticated and complex auditory telling and listening. For example, in 1995 Jodi Rose, an Australian sound artist, set out to record the sonic-scape, or sonic profile, of individual bridges around the world. After recording the unique 'sound signature' of Sydney's cable-stayed Glebe Island Bridge, she conceived a vast project, *Singing Bridges*, that would treat numerous major bridges around the world – including Brooklyn and Golden Gate in the USA, Tin Kau in Hong Kong and Tower Bridge in London – as instruments within a global bridge-orchestra. Drawn to the sound of wind through cables and struts, she attached microphones to them so they functioned as giant aeolian harps. Her vision was unashamedly spiritual. The wired-up bridge cables were conceived as echoing a globe-uniting and encircling, fibre-optic, telecommunications network. Jodi Rose imagined an 'International Bridge Symphony . . . A metaphor for spiritual communication'.[10]

There are also other, more discordant, even disturbing, soundings of the bridge, although few have been recorded: of construction and workers on the site; traffic noises; whispers, cries and metallic groans in the echoing spaces beneath the span or at its centre overhead; the screeching protest of its collapse or destruction. In the late 1980s, in the grey, damp, gloom of an English mid-winter, I would walk, generally feeling frustrated, to where the infamous M25, the London Orbital, had just been completed. The multi-lane highway, with a volume of traffic that always threatens to overwhelm its carrying capacity, was soon dubbed the world's longest traffic jam. It crossed over a small local road by means of a reinforced concrete bridge, already stained with atmospheric pollution. The endless rumbling of the traffic, overpowering in the confined space beneath the bridge, simply absorbed my therapeutic shouts. Iain Sinclair, documenting his idiosyncratic walk around the M25, says it better:

'We sit for a time under the Bulls Cross Bridge, watching the tide of traffic, the hallucinatory rush. Listening to the shift in the tyre sounds as the road surface changes, the thunderous amplification of the bridge.'[11] The experience summoned childhood memories: the Flying Scotsman powering its way north, smoke plume streaming, from King's Cross to Scotland, across a large steel bridge near my north London street. I would push against the huge sound rushing overhead, screaming through the iron and steel of the bridge. These sounds are more shamanic than spiritual, moving down and in, not out and up. Back to Sonny Rollins again, not just playing *on* the deserted places of the giant bridge but, as even a casual hearing of his bridge music suggests, playing *with* the bridge, playing *against* and *through* the complex and paradoxical structure.

Salginatobel Bridge, Switzerland, built 1929–30.

Engineering as story

The most obviously direct telling and representation of the bridge occurs within discourses of engineering – its manuals of analysis, design and project management. In his seminal 1979 study, *The Tower and the Bridge*, David Billington attempted to apply a critical reflexivity from within the engineering paradigm itself and hence to more fully understand and participate in the project of the modern bridge. He insisted upon a new perspective, 'a new art form, structural art, which is parallel to and fully independent of architecture'.[12] This was, he wrote, 'a new type of art – entirely the work of engineers and of the engineering imagination'.[13] A few engineers have 'consciously practised this art' since the late eighteenth century, but it was 'a movement awaiting a vocabulary'.[14]

Billington drew heavily upon the work of the twentieth-century Swiss bridge designer Robert Maillart as an exemplary case study in the development of structural art. Maillart, he insisted, 'was surely neither a sculptor nor architect: all of his works were rooted in the numerical rational world of engineering'.[15] Is bridge design and construction a science, a technology, or art, he asked. What is meant by such terms anyway? How have their meanings and significance, along with that of engineering or the engineer, changed, even throughout recent history?

The annals of structural and civil engineering are certainly full of disagreement and debate about how engineers should tell stories about bridges – the genres of analysis and design. Billington, while part of a minority, is not alone in his stress on the importance of historical understanding, particularly case studies. Indeed, nineteenth-century bridge designers drew deeply upon the history of various bridge designs, their failures and problems figuring strongly in their accounts. Billington suggests that an awareness of broad context,

THE NEW LONDON BRIDGE.
As it appeared on Monday August 1st 1831 at the Ceremony of opening by their Majesties.

THE TAY BRIDGE DISASTER—GENERAL VIEW OF THE DIVING OPERATIONS, LOOKING SOUTH

what he terms the 'climate of engineering design', is crucial. He links structural art to democratic society and its anti-totalitarian struggle: 'the disciplines of structural art are efficiency and economy, and its freedom lies in the potential it offers the individual designer for the expression of a personal style motivated by the conscious aesthetic search for engineering elegance.'[16]

Aesthetics and ethics are intractably linked in his vision: 'lightness, fragility perhaps – closely parallels the essence of a free and open society.'[17] This relationship between aesthetics and politics is

London Bridge opening by King William IV, on 15 August 1831.

The Tay Bridge Disaster, Scotland, 28 December 1879.

crucial. For Billington, the bridge seems simultaneously to condense and amplify entire political cultures and ideologies. The bridge is both a key cipher for interpreting politics and culture, plus a technology of change and affirmation: 'The thinness and openness of the Eiffel Tower, Brooklyn Bridge, and Maillart's arches . . . have a deep affinity to both the political traditions and era in which they arose. They symbolize the artificial rather than the natural, the democratic rather than the autocratic and the transparent rather than the impenetrable.'[18] London Bridge of 1831, by comparison, built of solid masonry, was both costly and monumental, a product of a less democratic and open society, one that was more hierarchical, more autocratic and aristocratic. Billington particularly focused on the Menai suspension bridge of 1826 by Thomas Telford. It was, he wrote, 'the first major work of structural art visually to symbolize, in its thinness, the lightness of the new engineering and the demands of the new politics'.[19] This bridge was contemporaneous with the Reform Bill of 1832, and the struggle to spread the franchise in Britain. Among other bridge-designing social radicals and revolutionaries of the time was Thomas Paine, who combined a dedication to structures and politics. Paine described his seminal work *The Rights of Man* as his political bridge. For Billington there is a direct connection between a revolution in bridge technology and politics.

The emergence of new materials in structural engineering, such as iron, steel and concrete, are used by Billington to date shifts in the fundamental design of bridges and their construction. For him the modern begins in 1779 with Abraham Darby III's Iron Bridge at Coalbrookedale in England and the use of cast iron for complete structures: 'new structural forms began to appear; these required special study and training, which led to the creation of the modern engineering profession.'[20] This is clearly an engineering view of the initiatory moment for the birth of the modern bridge, but provides a useful historical starting point for this book. Other perspectives provide different opening dates – the emergence of new mobilities, radical shifts of perspective in art, new flows of imperialism and capital that demanded innovative systems of communications, major changes in social relations, and so on. Darby's bridge looked backwards in its design, not just to an established arch-form that had evolved for more traditional materials but to established social relationships and mobilities. The modern bridge can be considered not just as an engineering structure, nor as defining a moment in engineering history, but, for example, as a platform for a certain kind of reverie on the modern city. In this regard we could point to Wordsworth's poetry, firstly to his 'Ode on Westminster Bridge', with its elegiac celebration of London, and then to his various drafts of *The Prelude* with their more sombre, even disillusioned, appraisal.[21] Billington's insistence that the 'development of the new technology of industrial iron brought forth a new means of artistic expression', should go beyond just bridge design to embrace the 'artistic imagination', as he puts it, of an entire era.[22]

Unquestionably the advent of railways, a complex and multi-causal event in its own right, was the force that galvanized the development of the modern bridge. There was pressure to use as few natural resources as possible because of their cost, particularly industrialized iron. The immensely higher loading on bridges due to locomotives, the demand for longer spans in order to provide the most direct route for ever-expanding transportation systems, each pushed the boundaries of design. The modern bridge as a form of structural art emerged, as engineers struggled to find both the limits of structure and also forms that were not just light but which conspicuously displayed their lightness.[23]

For Billington, the second period of the modern bridge started in the 1880s when iron was supplanted, and largely replaced, by steel and then concrete. This allowed an extraordinary range of design options and a bewildering variety of bridge forms came into being. But conservative powers still prevailed and it has been noted that there were no courses in steel and concrete construction in architectural education for the new engineering. Significantly, for Billington's compelling thesis, Thomas Telford, one of the pioneers of structural art, had taken a strong stand for independence of engineering from both eighteenth-century architecture and eighteenth-century mathematics.

However, at the beginning of the twentieth century mathematics and science were highly prestigious and began to dominate bridge design. Petroski is critical of such developments, insisting that 'highly developed analytical, numerical, and computational design tools' are not enough.[24] Like Billington, he stresses the importance for engineers of developing case studies, of knowing history, of an awareness of failure and its causes, of understanding the social, historical and ideological contexts of bridges. Petroski approvingly cites one designer: 'problems are essentially nonquantitative . . . solutions are essentially non-numerical.'[25] There is an unavoidable fuzziness in trying to define engineering method. He too points to the example of the Swiss engineer Robert Maillart, who, in 1923, 'developed a limited theory for one of his arch bridge types that violated in principle the general mathematical theory of structures.'[26] But during the twentieth century many were 'trapped in a view of an engineering analysis which was so complex that it obscured new design possibilities. Today the undue reliance on complex computer analysis can have the same limiting effect on design.'[27]

The key issue here is how a cluster of professions and practices such as engineers and engineering, architects and architecture, have

been understood across history. Designers such as Robert Maillart and Santiago Calatrava, whose bridges receive direct acclaim as modern art, are in the forefront of challenging any rigid classifications.[28]

The extreme possibilities in the telling of a bridge are boldly illustrated by comparing two radically different narratives about the Dartford crossing which opened in 1991, a huge cable-stayed bridge with a main span of 450 metres over the Thames. One is the rather bland, celebratory description using generic promotional-technical rhetoric as told by the company operating what is officially called the Queen Elizabeth II Bridge, and the other is the underworld vision of poet and writer Iain Sinclair on his bizarre walk around the M25.

Calatrava's Alamillo Bridge, Seville, Spain, opened 1992.

For the operating company the bridge is, understandably, a technical structure deserving of celebration:

> Now as you travel along the approach roads towards the Dartford River crossing the new Bridge rises dramatically into view, the largest and most dominant feature on the horizon. Slender steel pylons rise from the road deck 137 metres into the sky above the river. Immensely strong galvanized spiral strand cables are anchored down the height of each pylon and connect along the length of the road deck, forming a graceful sweep of steel strands that, when seen from a distance, seem no more than fine threads to the eye.[29]

By contrast, Sinclair's rich, gritty underworld perspective locates the bridge in a lived context:

> Heading east, along the Thames path, the Dartford Bridge (with its necklace of slow-moving traffic) is our horizon. Smeared headlights spit their short beams into the wet night. The bridge spells civilization. And it spells it loud: FUCK OFF. Liminal graffiti. A mess of letters sprayed on grey stone wind-breaks. FUCK OFF . . . The motorway streaks the land with sick light. For half a mile, in every direction, there is hard evidence: burnt-out wrecks, torched and rusting husks, solitary tyres. The trash of transit . . . The sewerage plant hums and seethes . . . Mythic projections invade an unoptioned landscape, the gloom over Gravesend. The bridge is more metaphor than reality, lorries disappear into the clouds.[30]

The clean promotional language in the first account depersonalizes the bridge. The viewpoint is at a distance. By contrast Sinclair's perspective is close up, figuratively in-your-face. The bridge is grubby from use. It is integrated into the harsh life of the road and city. The prose is a challenge to the incorporation of bridges into a vision of progress that celebrates an almost dematerialized world of free-flowing transportation and global capital, a view that ignores the inevitable creation of a complex and messy underworld. The two accounts are like the ultra-violet and infra-red ends of a spectrum of stories a bridge evokes.

Gendered bridges

Social class and ethnicity are critical to stories about the bridge. But the voices of the vast historical labour force, involved in

Workers on the cables of Brooklyn Bridge, 1883.

bridging – from design offices to construction and maintenance – have at best been pushed to the margins, while at worst they are simply effaced. The workers remain enigmatically fixed as anonymous figures in the documentary images of the construction or as statistics (4,600 employed on the Forth Bridge construction between 1883 and 1890, with 57 killed). Subsequent chapters begin to explore the power equation, including racist ones, inherent in the telling of bridges. Gender too is inextricably part of the telling. Structural or civil engineering has long been blatantly gendered as a male domain. Back in the mid-1960s when I studied Civil Engineering at a major university in England, out of about 300 first-year engineering students rumour had it that only one was female. While the rates of participation by women in civil and structural engineering vary quite significantly from one country to the next, these professions have always been overwhelmingly dominated by men. With varying success moves have been taken in recent years by engineering organizations and in universities around the world to correct this gross imbalance.

It is difficult to say how the history of structural design/art would have been different if there had been a more equitable gender balance among those who designed and built. However, even the few women who have played crucial roles in bridge design and construction are usually quietly pushed out of sight. Emily Roebling's critical part in the completion of Brooklyn Bridge, for example, took a long time to receive due acknowledgement. After the bridge had killed its prime designer, John Roebling, his son, Washington, had assumed responsibility. Then he too was severely incapacitated by the bridge, permanently crippled by the 'bends' or 'caisson disease' during construction of the foundations. His wife Emily then took over, going far beyond the role of mere go-between or messenger for her house-bound husband that many have assigned her. In Alan Trachtenberg's seminal 1965 book on the Brooklyn Bridge, Emily warrants just a single brief mention, and then merely as her crippled husband's courier. Others have insisted that she taught herself higher mathematics and the details of engineering in order better to interpret her husband's plans, ideas and notes for his associates. She was therefore in a position to explain the difficult points and directly examine the results.[31]

A more recent example of the belittling of women who have been involved in a major bridging project is that of Marilyn Jorgenson Reece and Carol Schumaker. They designed the complex cluster of bridges that, when completed in 1964, constituted one of the busiest intersections in the world, the San Diego/Santa Monica Freeway interchange in Los Angeles.[32] A headline in the *LA Times* of 6 April 1964 read: 'Freeway Builders Are Weekend Housewives: Highway Engineers Look Forward to Ordinary Suburban Chores Around Home.' Nevertheless, the legacy of these engineers remains and the Santa Monica/San Diego intersection has been described as 'a work of art, both as a pattern on the map, as a monument against

Fireworks on the Tsing Ma Bridge, Hong Kong, at the official opening of the Lantau Link.

the sky, and as a kinetic experience as one sweeps through it'.[33] Fictional portrayals of women bridge-builders are few. Frank Worsdale has two of them – one Chinese and one British – in his novel about a plot by Islamic terrorists (based in Afghanistan) to blow up the giant Tsing Ma Bridge, a celebrated Hong Kong icon.[34]

Of course women claim a place in the telling of bridges in other ways. Sydney Harbour Bridge has been the focus of celebrated women artists, such as Grace Cossington-Smith, Dorrit Black and Gwen Barringer, since its construction phase. Bridges have also been the site of contention by women, from city planners and urban environmentalists such as Jane Jacobs in the 1960s, to ongoing struggles over the right of women to safe mobility in city streets.[35] Bridges have not always been seen by women as simply beneficial. As will be seen in Chapter One, Aboriginal women in South Australia were at the forefront of desperate attempts in the 1980s to block approval for a bridge that they insisted would inflict devastating damage to their sacred landscape around Hindmarsh Island.[36]

George Cruikshank, plate 8 of the series *The Drunkard's Children*, 1848.

Young women in trouble, framed by the underside of the bridge, have long been a favourite of (male) artists, particularly in the Victorian era, as in George Cruikshank's *The Drunkard's Children*, or his explicitly titled 1848 painting, *The Poor girl, homeless, friendless, deserted and gin mad, commits self-murder* or in George Frederic Watts's 1850 painting, *Found Drowned*, or Gustave Doré's 1872 engraving of a young woman, presumably drowned, lying beside the Thames beneath a London bridge. Young women seem to outnumber young men or older people of any gender in artistic portrayals of bridge-related suicides. Intricate complexities – ideological, political, psychological, cultural and social – of gender and technology require careful attention, as they do around all social inequalities which circulate around a technology of power like the bridge.[37]

New spaces

The story about Sonny Rollins playing his sax on the walkway of Williamsburg Bridge bypasses and relativizes the narrative genres of engineering triumph and architectural aesthetics, of documentary or artistic visuality. Span and mobility are pushed to the very

Praying on Williamsburg Bridge, on New Year's Day, 1909.

Sunset from Williamsburg Bridge, 1915, etching.

VIEW OF LONDON,
(FROM WATERLOO BRIDGE)

edge of the frame as other spaces and functions are moved to the centre. It opens up a very different telling of the bridge, one enunciated from marginalized, or even subaltern, spacialities. These marginalized spaces are sometimes transgressive, sometimes demonized, generally problematic.

Over the past two hundred years bridges have been involved in creating new, often paradoxical, spaces as well as new practices, experiences and imaginings of place. At the most local of levels this has involved the bridge structure itself. Most obvious is the span with its centre – the highest point, the crown of the bridge, the desperate leap, the point of reverie, the place of transformation in myth and folk tales, the site of prayer. In an earlier age, to stand on the crown of a large bridge was the closest one could get to flight: surrounded by space, suspended high in space, supported only by a minimum of matter.

A view of Blackfriars Bridge from Waterloo Bridge, London, in 1832.

As a platform from which to view, the bridge also opens up another entirely new type of space and subjectivity. Not only does it introduce a unique viewing position, a kind of *offing* is also created, akin to the place revealed by the glance from a ship at anchor, or from the shore over an arc comprising the visible stretch of sea. The bridge becomes a platform for reverie, or for a gaze either critical or admiring, or for survey and surveillance. From Dostoevsky in St Petersburg to Wordsworth in London, the viewing from the bridge is also implicated in a struggle over certain kinds of subjectivity and identity.[38] In Andric's novel, *The Bridge on the Drina*, the middle of the bridge over the Drina in Bosnia plays an important role.[39] Here the bridge widened into two terraces – the *kapia*. It was a place where men (rarely women) used to meet over coffee, to contemplate the river and life. It was a pivotal place in the town's geography and everyday coherence.

There are also the ends, the entrance and exit (the approaches, the sense of initiation, of defence, of entry and departure). Shops, hotels, cafes and dwellings gathered around the ends of many earlier, and even some modern, bridges.

Finally, there is the space beneath the bridge (the place of secrets, of trolls and tramps, a refuge for wanderers and homeless, a site of crimes, graffiti, the damp smell of water, earth, stone and

The approaches to Brooklyn Bridge, 1881.

concrete, of urine, faeces and of hasty sex). Bridges gather to themselves an underside. To construct a bridge is always to construct an underworld. This is a place of stillness and exile, a world of alternative aesthetic possibilities as well as devalued real-estate.

Road Bridge over Fourth Creek, Morialta, South Australia.

Gustave Doré, 'Under the Bridges', from *London: A Pilgrimage* (1872).

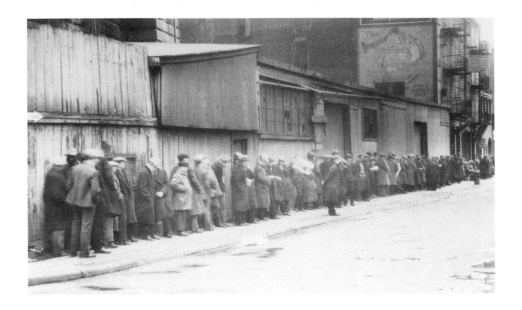

It is outside the rush and flow taking place above, over the bridge. There is something about bridges as a whole that is uncanny, but this uncanniness is at its maximum in the spaces beneath the span. The underside of bridges is both a literal and metaphorical under-world. It can act as a potent frame as in Edward Hopper's sketch of 1906–09, *On the Quai: Suicide*, where the arch of the bridge looms in the background and a solitary viewer stares from the bridge at the small group gathering around an ill-defined corpse, or in the Depression-era photo of a line of men queuing for food beneath a bridge in the USA.[40] This underside also encompasses the shady deals surrounding bridge constructions, the financial and power play that lies behind many bridges, the misuse of place and environment by a cult of speed, circulation and unrestrained mobility. It also acts as a potent metaphor that has been utilized by artists, poets, writers, philosophers and filmmakers, and acts as

Breadline at McCauley Water Street Mission under Brooklyn Bridge, 1930s.

a sobering counter to the idealistic visions that accompany the soaring span. The construction of any bridge or, I would argue, just the imagining of any bridge, creates an underworld, an inevitable and essential shadow side.

Bridges also affect the immediate gathering of the lands and cultures around them. On a larger scale bridges are involved in the creation of extensive and often global corridors of transportation, communication and power, as well as a reconfiguration of border and territory. Bridges, perhaps more than any other single structure, radically alter the face of a landscape. A massive redistribution of imaginative and social space can result from the construction of a major bridge. This was part of their attraction to early visionary designers. Offices, factories, homes, shops, roads and parks spring up and gather in relationship to a new bridge. There is a shift in the centre of gravity of a landscape, sometimes on a vast scale. Brooklyn Bridge, for example, was conceived as being at the centre of a shift of civilization itself, away from Europe and towards America. Such structures, their eco-imaginative location placed within a broad physical and social context, contribute to the *genius loci* of a landscape. But for many people construction was and is experienced as an imposition, as destruction, an expression of the power of others and of their own powerlessness. As will be seen in subsequent chapters, bridges can focus a considerable disturbance from afar onto a local place and, more often than is acknowledged, stimulate resistance.

At one extreme, bridges create complex places that can be intricate and intimate, social or solitary. At the other they seem to create places of homogenized desolation. In between they are perhaps what Marc Augé has called non-places, ones without the usual defining characteristics of a relationship to meaningful everyday life, or to history, or to concerns with identity.[41] Spaces

of transportation, from aircraft cabins to airports, highways to high-speed trains, are particularly in Augé's sights. Yet, as will be seen, even apparently nondescript bridges, vast and complex multi level highway intersections that devour bridges and land,

London Bridge, 1833.

derelict undersides of bridges, are often not devoid of meaning, of life. Such gargantuan interchanges, for example, have their own devotees and fans.[42] As already mentioned, Reyner Banham, while critical of many highway interchanges, admires others, such as the Santa Monica/San Diego intersection, insisting it is 'a work of art'.[43] The exit points of such complexes, where the ramps link to other orders of flow, can be sites where hitchers thumb for lifts, kerbside vendors proffer flowers, or carjackers and thieves lurk. The spaces beneath can provide shelter.

There are also small, intimate spaces and corners within and around the bridge. Numerous poets, novelists and filmmakers

Aerial view of four-level interchange at intersection of Arroyo Seco Parkway and Highway 101, Hollywood Freeway.

invoke a poetics of such spaces, and suggest reverie as a way of apprehending the bridge.[44] Bridges are places of meeting, sites of loss and of parting. As in the 1940s film *Waterloo Bridge*, or the 1991 film *Lovers on the Bridge*, in Guillaume Apollinaire's wistfully graceful poem 'Mirabeau Bridge' lovers eternally meet at the centre of bridges, either physically or in solitary thought, lonely, in moments of reflection:[45]

> Under the Mirabeau Bridge there flows the Seine
>> Must I recall
> Our loves recall how then
> After each sorrow joy came back again . . .

The intimate bridge is a technology of possibilities. It is a place where tragedy or just sadness always hovers. Memory, nostalgia, dreams and intimacy have long haunted bridges.[46] Romanticism, the picturesque, psychoanalysis, surrealism, the rhetorical strategies of heritage and tourist promotion, of Feng Shui and garden landscape design, as well as a postmodern irony, have provided just a few of the changing genres within which and around which such sentiments have been mobilized and contested. This is a world of glimpses, of bits of bridges, of meetings and partings.

Psycho-philosophical bridges

Bridges have long attracted the attention of philosophers, theologians and psychologists. One of the earliest psychoanalysts, Sandor Ferenczi, gave a rich, albeit highly reductive, interpretation of the bridge as a symbol. In 'dreams of neurotics', he wrote, 'the bridge is the male organ, and in particular the powerful organ of the father, which unites two landscapes (the two parents in the giant shapes in which they appear to the infant view). This bridge spans a wide and perilous stream, from which all life takes its origin . . .'[47] He pointed to 'the two meanings "bridge = uniting member between the parents" and bridge = link between life and not-life (death)'.[48] The 'bridge anxiety' is hence a fear of castration: 'The male member which unites the parents during intercourse, and to which the little child must cling if it is not to perish in the "deep water" across which the bridge is thrown', is 'an important vehicle between the "Beyond" (the condition of the unborn, the womb) and the "Here" (life)'.[49] For Ferenczi, the bridge is also a key symbol of the pathway to death, echoing T. S. Eliot's portrayal in *Four Quartets* of London Bridge as a passageway for the dead.[50]

The constant tension between the physicality and symbolism of the bridge was remarked upon by Heidegger, who insisted that 'the bridge, if it is a true bridge, is never first of all a mere bridge and then afterward a symbol. And just as little is the bridge in the first place exclusively a symbol.'[51] Heidegger wrote that bridges are 'things', *thingness* being the capacity to initiate a fourfold gathering of earth, sky, divinities and mortals. In a famous passage he explained:

> The bridge swings over the stream with ease and power. It does not just connect banks that are already there, the banks emerge as banks only as the bridge crosses the stream . . . With the banks, the bridge brings to the stream the expanse of the landscape lying behind them. It brings stream and bank and land into each other's neighbourhood. The bridge gathers the earth as landscape around the stream.[52]

Bridges initiate a paradoxical gathering. They are also quintessential technologies of separating and of separation. Around the turn of the century, the classic sociologist and social philosopher Georg Simmel also reflected on the bridge. Humans, by their very nature,

he suggested, 'separate the connected or connect the separate'.[53] Simmel emphasized the bridge's place within what he called 'the miracle of the road: freezing movement into a solid structure'.[54] Within an overall structure of movement the bridge gives visible form to this rhythm of separating and connecting.

The bridge as a technology

Obviously a study of bridges must engage with the idea of technology. In this book I use the word technology not to indicate just a thing, a means or a process, but as a way of knowing, or, in Heidegger's phrase, 'a way of revealing'.[55] For Heidegger, technology 'actively "enframes" or "emplaces" (Gestell) an aspect of the world'.[56] He uses the example of a power station on the Rhine – a complex assemblage of various technologies that reveal the river Rhine in a very specific way, very different from, for example,

Bridge over the Rhine at Coblenz, c. 1890–1900.

myth or poetry. Similarly, a bridge, whether ancient or modern, over the Rhine provides another way in which the river is revealed. The problem for Heidegger is that technology's 'mode of revealing the world destroys other possible ways of revealing'.[57] One possible solution is to embrace a fuller meaning of *techne*, one that 'often had little to do with the "enframing technology"', echoing Billington's call for a structural art of bridge design.[58]

I use the term 'technology' in a way that indicates both an instrumental means, a technique, tool or apparatus, a systems of sciences, and also a regime of practices, a complex world of meanings, of social relationships. It suggests a culture which supports, even encourages, attempts at systematic transformation and systematic applied knowledge. It also indicates a specific type of enframing of the world, posits certain goals, valorizes certain actions, shapes aesthetics, establishes a mythology and a poetics. Technology is, as Robert Romanyshyn eloquently puts it, both symptom and dream.[59]

Bridge biographies

In the telling of bridges the auteurs of design and construction receive star billing. Individual designers such as Brunel, Roebling, Telford, Eiffel, Lindenthal, Ammann, Maillart, Calatrava, and Armajani have an obviously compelling relationship to specific bridges and to the historical narrative about the structural art of bridge-building. But the Sonny Rollins story also introduces other biographical dimensions to the telling of the bridge. A range of people, such as artists, poets, musicians, general users and 'fans', or those in design offices, or construction workers, can also have an intensely personal relationship to bridges. Their stories are heard less often.

Old London Bridge, moved from London to Lake Havasu City, Mohave County, Arizona.

Signa Bridge near Florence being destroyed by Allied bombers in World War II.

Bridges too have their own biography. As Igor Koptoff insists, things have a social life, a complex story that changes across their life spans. Culture and history utterly transform the context of a bridge.[60] The meanings and functions of bridges are not fixed. An out-of-date rail bridge can give up its original function and instead, in a new era of heritage, environment and fitness, become part of a pedestrian and cycling trail. Bridges even change their structure as elements are added or removed, parts strengthened, carriageways widened. Bridges can become non-functional monuments, themed and landscaped as picturesque ruins, or protected and framed as heritage. Over two hundred years after its completion the seminal Iron Bridge stands at the centre of a historical themed open-air museum. The famed bridge over the River Kwai at Kanchanaburi in Thailand has been transformed from imperial death sentence for war prisoners to a site for tourists and pilgrims.[61] London Bridge's transformation was even more dramatic. Closed after 140 years of use, both functionally and as iconic image of early twentieth-century London, a bustling heart of global finance, trade and entertainment, it was auctioned in 1968. Bought by an American entrepreneur, it was dismantled stone by stone, transported and reassembled in a desert, an instant improbable icon for a city planned and created only in 1963, Lake Havasu City, Arizona.

Australian postage stamp commemorating the 2000 Sydney Olympics.

The bridge as stage and target

The use of the bridge, such as Sydney Harbour's, as an immense and highly visible stage for enacting mass spectaculars, is merely the other side of an equation that sees bridges as targets – whether in wars, guerrilla actions or in an era of terrorist threat.

Behind the populist appeals of spectacular firework displays lies corporate–national–civic power and aspiration. From Sydney Harbour to Hong Kong's Tsing Ma, bridges are not just being integrated into the branding of cities and nations, also they are often the *key* branding icon used on everything from postage stamps to nationalistic tourist advertisements. The third phase of the modern bridge, the postmodern bridge, could be said to start after the conclusion of the Second World War. Its genesis can be traced not only to the advent of new materials, new techniques of computation, construction and manufacture, but also to a totally new milieu of globalization and promotionality.

Bridges also have long functioned as quasi-billboards. Winter driving in England down the M1 reveals desperate signs on grim concrete overpass bridges, barely legible through a windscreen covered with grey drizzle and the muck-saturated spray of passing trucks: 'Give me inspiration', or the more ubiquitous 'Jesus Saves'.

Invisible bridges

The countless numbers of small, unprepossessing, mundane bridges that are essential to the communication and transportation networks around the globe – the structurally small but socially significant links so crucial to numberless communities – are often ignored. Glossy photo-illustrated books with titles such as *Bridges that Changed the World* or *Bridges: Three Thousand Years of Defying*

Nature or *Bridges: A History of the World's Most Famous and Important Spans*, while visually exciting, pay scant attention – like haute couture in fashion or haute cuisine in food – to the small details of everyday life and its engagement with bridges both large and small.[62]

Bridges have been silently incorporated into the transportation systems of modernity and postmodernity, from vast, complex and often bewildering motorway interchanges (each of which literally devour dozens of bridges whilst simultaneously rendering them invisible) to small individual rail and highway bridges, foot-bridges, as well as bridges that are invisible in their bridge-ness – viaducts, culverts, underpasses.

Complex, multilevel interchanges have been around since 1858, when Olmsted built an overpass to separate intersecting traffic in New York's Central Park. The first cloverleaf interchange was built near Woodbridge, New Jersey in 1928. The imperative behind the

Bridges over an autobahn, late 1930s.

design and construction of modern freeways from the 1920s onwards – such as the 1924 Du Pont Highway in Delaware, the first limited access road in the USA, or the revolutionary German autobahn – was the demand for free-flowing, uninterrupted traffic movement. The fantasy of speed and flow which came to dominate road design also captured the bridge, which became subservient to the road.

The entrances and exits to bridges were traditionally places to pause and where buildings gathered. Now, unless they are quickly forced to stop at a toll booth, it is illegal for drivers to pause at such places. Many large bridges scarcely have any provision for pedestrians. Roebling's insistence on a separate walkway for pedestrians across Brooklyn Bridge in 1883, on which they could pause and breathe the clean air, almost marked the end of an era.

An autobahn with service station and bridge, late 1930s.

On the Promenade, Brooklyn Bridge, New York,
Copyright 1899 by Strohmeyer & Wyman.

The bridge as accident

Lev Zetlin philosophically commented, 'I look at everything and try to imagine disaster'.[63] As Paul Virilio has suggested, every technological advance is simultaneously the invention of a new form of accident. The railway accident is integral to the invention of railways, automobile accidents to the invention of the automobile, and so on. A whole culture of disaster clusters around, weaves its way through, any technological 'advance'. Certainly the bridge accident is not entirely new, but in the industrial age such events assumed new, often catastrophic dimensions. The collapse of the Dee Bridge in Scotland in 1847 was the one of the first such disasters of a large metal railway bridge, but the Tay Bridge collapse of 1879 – when a whole section of the bridge, along with a complete train full of passengers, disappeared one stormy Scottish night – came to haunt the construction of long-span railway bridges in the immediate aftermath. Extra strengthening and over-design became the standard practice, admittedly sometimes producing masterpieces such as the Forth Bridge or Roebling's suspension

On the promenade, Brooklyn Bridge, c. 1899.

bridge at Niagara Falls. From the disaster of Quebec Bridge in 1907 to the well-filmed spectacular and tortured demise of the Tacoma Narrows suspension bridge in 1940 in the USA, the collapse of a bridge is a major and very specific event. So frequent were the collapse of major bridges in the early years of the nineteenth century that it became the focus of a well-recognized phobia.

With the invention of the modern bridge has also come the development of new kinds of danger, risk and accident. The bridge, while so much an image of hope and possibility, therefore also takes its place within the changing landscape of a modern risk society.

There is a tendency to focus on the spectacular in all aspects of bridges – whether immense spans, dramatic locations, audacious designs or calamitous disasters. But, as with most troubles associated with specific technologies, the majority of those associated with bridges are small, albeit no less significant or potentially less dangerous. Bridge closures, collapses and failures of one sort or another are a regular feature of the global bridge-scape. Unlike any other structure, bridges by their very nature are prone to some kind of 'collapse'. In 1995 the US Department of Transportation warned, 'The continued economic strength and growth of the United States is intimately linked to the strength and reliability of our highways and bridges. The American public is experiencing the effects of an aging and deteriorating highway system . . . [D]eteriorating bridges are becoming more severe choke points in the system.'[64] The message is clear: corrosion, fatigue and lack of maintenance and inspection result at best in non-functioning bridges, and at worst in collapse, death and injury. In 1992 the cost of repairing the backlog of bridge deficiencies in the US was estimated to be almost $80 billion. The bill simply to maintain the condition of the bridges was estimated at over $8 billion. Current funding fell considerably short of this amount. According to one 1980s report, 'every other day, a bridge falls, sags or buckles somewhere in the US'.[65] It points out that two out of five of the 524,966 bridges in the USA needed major repairs or replacements. The effort and cost involved in the maintenance of bridges can be astronomical.

As well as structural malfunctions, bridge disasters also encompass social calamities: deaths in crushing, panicking crowds such as at the opening of Brooklyn Bridge; financial scams; and cost blowouts.

Vectorial politics and technologies of power

Bridges have long and widely been used as technologies of power within political, social and cultural landscapes. The contemporary bridge construction programme being undertaken by the Beijing government, in its mission to accelerate the incorporation, occu-

George Westinghouse Bridge, Spanning Turtle Creek at Lincoln Highway (US Route 30), East Pittsburgh, Pennsylvania, c. 1968.

pation, domination and control of Tibet, has its precedent 250 years ago when the governments of England and lowland Scotland put extensive bridge construction in the vanguard of their intent similarly to control the Scottish Highlands, its culture and its people, at best to harness its productive potential, or at worst to neutralize them as a threat. Shifting paradigms of power circulate through and around bridges.

Two key vectors created within a bridge – across the span (horizontality) and up–down (verticality) – are in constant tension, even contradiction. When involved in a politics of horizontality and of extension bridges are key technologies for vast transportation and communication systems. With the bridge as border it becomes a technology of separation as well as one, normally emphasized, of connection. As border technology the bridge controls flow and access, separates out the mobility-rich and mobility-poor.

While this border function usually occurs across a horizontal boundary, it can be vertical, in what Eyal Weizman has called a politics of verticality, the use of bridges physically and symbolically not only to assert power and status, but to inscribe them in space and place.[66] Eugene Levy has succinctly discussed the way in which two bridges in Pittsburgh illustrate this purpose.[67] George Westinghouse Bridge is a high bridge, physically, culturally, socially, and symbolically, while Wall Bridge is a similarly low one. The monumental, concrete spans of Westinghouse Bridge dominate the landscape. Wall Bridge, however, covered in graffiti, is a downbeat steel structure. Both were built in the early twentieth century. The high bridge was named after the man who built the famous factory in the 1890s that employed thousands in its best years. A huge steel mill was located next door. In the 1920s travellers on the main US Highway 30 had to drive down into a steep-sided valley through the noisy, crowded and polluted indus-

trial zone. In 1931 the high bridge was built, 460 metres across and 60 metres high, over the Turtle Creek Valley. With bold bass-reliefs inscribed at each end celebrating an idealized techno-triumph-antism, it dominated the town and effectively created a vertical separation in terms of social class. Travellers could pause and scan the town from above, thereby avoiding the industrial atmosphere and working-class people of the valley. By contrast, Wall Bridge, down in the valley, is gritty and small. It gives an eye-level view

George Westinghouse Bridge, East Pittsburgh.

of industrial landscape. Once extensively used by workers going to and from the factories, the graffiti which covers it was once sentimental. Now, in an era of factory closure and unemployment it is mainly confrontational.

There is always a power equation associated with bridges. This can be manifested merely through the name, as was the case with the Verrazano Narrows Bridge.[68] In 1524 Verrazano, sailing on orders from Francis I, King of France, became the first European to encounter what is now New York harbour. He was an overlooked explorer, due the prominence given to Henry Hudson (and eventual British colonization of the region). Anti-Italian prejudice was blamed for not naming the bridge after him; others said his name was simply too long. Even after opening in 1964 the bridge was often just called 'the Narrows Bridge', or the Brooklyn/Staten

Verrazano-Narrows Bridge from Brooklyn, opened 1964.

Island Bridge. The Italian Historical Society worked hard to ensure its proper name is now commonly used. Here was a tale of multi-culturalism and the struggles between the historical narratives of rival colonizing powers. The underdog, 'ethnic' connection to the bridge was mobilized in the classic 1977 film *Saturday Night Fever*, which opens with a beautiful shot of the Brooklyn Bridge as seen from the Brooklyn side, which looks dreary by comparison. Tony, the young working-class Italian-American protagonist, is uncomfortable with the glamorous Manhattan over the bridge. Brooklyn Bridge is portrayed as a no-go zone that separates social and ethnic groups. Tony and his gang feel more comfortable with Verrazano Narrows Bridge connecting Brooklyn to Staten Island and that is the one they use. The two bridges are referred to constantly, both visually and in dialogue, as symbols of dreams, hopes, memories and anxieties.

Bridge as crossing

In the context of pilgrimage the Sanskrit word *Tirtha* means a crossing, both geographical and symbolically. It indicates both a physical movement across an obstacle such as a river and a spiritual-psychological movement between two different orders of reality and experience.[69] A bridge always creates a crossing, indeed is a technology of crossing. For Sonny Rollins the bridge allowed a crossing from one problematic emotional/creative situation to another far more satisfying one. Bridges are sites where disparate tracks cross – transportation, communication, cultural and social, environmental and aesthetic.

Bridges mark a different time scale and rhythm to individual human life. With their longevity and the unique sense of almost sacredness with which they are often associated, they can impart an intimation of immortality – like great cathedrals, temples and mosques. The bridge as a whole is a liminal space, a transition, a border, a place in-between.[70] Mythologically this in-between-ness was expressed as something numinous and paradoxical: the rainbow bridge of the gods, *Bifrost*, and the golden-paved bridge, *Gjallarbru*, in Nordic mythology; the Chinvat bridge in Iranian mythology over which the dead must pass – nine lengths wide for the good and just, but as narrow as the blade of a razor for the wicked. Along with hope comes hopelessness.

The bridge was imagined to define a place between life and death, the sacred and the profane, the worlds of gods and of humans. For some this in-between-ness is a kind of limbo, a nowhere place. In Iain Banks's disturbingly surreal modern novel, *The Bridge*, the protagonist enters a coma after a near-fatal accident but then finds himself in a strange, nightmarish landscape, a world constituted almost entirely by a bridge that stretches beyond both horizons.[71] Time and space are suspended, along with normal laws. People inhabit the bridge and live out their lives without leaving it. Indeed, there seems to be no way off the bridge.

The 1970 best-selling song by Simon and Garfunkel, 'Bridge Over Troubled Water', resonated against a rich landscape of metaphor and symbol. Bridges are structures for the performance of connection and gathering, hope and reconciliation, as well as of division, separation and antagonism. Recent mass walks over the Sydney Harbour Bridge and over those in every capital city, calling for social justice and reconciliation between indigenous and non-indigenous Australians, must be placed alongside the deliberate targeting of bridges elsewhere either for symbolic destruction or blockade. Numerous so-called 'Friendship bridges' around the world signal optimism and perhaps desperate hope. The changing contexts of such crossings and divisions, whether military, economic or social, need to be explored.

These include the shifting meaning and purpose of 'taking to the streets' and occupying bridges. Mass demonstrations on contemporary highways have new meaning in our era of online global flows and mass air transportation.

The sense of paradoxical crossing is crucial. In the religious-philosophizing of Thornton Wilder's classic novel of the 1930s, *The Bridge of San Luis Rey*, the collapse of a bridge in Peru and the resulting death of five people becomes the focus of a priest's inquiry into the dilemma between random chance and a cosmic order based upon the judgement of God.[72] The choice is boldly defined. Attempts are made to exclude paradox from the equation. On the other hand, Hölderlin, in his 1802 poem, 'Patmos', tries to embrace it:[73]

> Near is
> The God and hard to grasp,
> But where there is danger,
> The saving powers go too.
> In darkness dwell
> The eagles, and fearless across
> The abyss go the sons of the Alps
> On lightly built bridges.

In *Thus Spoke Zarathustra* (1883) Nietzsche imagined humanity as a rope, stretched between the beast and the superman – and spanning an abyss. It was a perilous crossing and it was dangerous to look back; any hesitation was disastrous and treacherous. Humanity is great because a human being is a bridge and not a goal, fit to be loved only when in transition and a failure.[74]

Bridges, along with tunnels and ferries, constitute the core technologies of crossings and their associated activities: bridging; tunnelling; ferrying. Each has their specific field of associations and symbology. While awesome and uncanny, tunnels lack the affection given to ferries and bridges. They also lack their spiritual associations. Even bridges can want for the nostalgic associations so often given to ferries. Bridges cross *over*; tunnels cross *under*; ferries go *across*. The symbolic strength and physical quality of what is being crossed by the bridge is also crucial: The Rhine; Victoria Falls; Niagara Falls; Sydney Harbour; the Mississippi; the Seine; the Thames; the Ganges.

Time and again, in the examples that are elaborated in the following chapters, it will be seen how a bridge condenses and displaces, almost as if in a Freudian dream process, complex and often contradictory narratives. For example, in the Victorian British

Brooklyn Bridge, New York, from the Manhattan Bridge.

painting *Past and Present, Number 3* (1858), Augustus Egg portrays a highly moralistic and melodramatic view of the terrible consequences of a wife's infidelity. The distraught 'guilty' woman, exiled from her home, is shown taking shelter under a bridge near the Strand in London. The underside of the bridge is mobilized, with all its complex connotations and associations. The painting condenses the realities and the fantasies about the Victorian city, ideas about gender, morality, power, of melodramatic moralizing and genuine social concern. The powerless plight of women under Victorian patriarchy is displaced into the underside of the bridge, which becomes a site of punishment and refuge, perhaps a site also of remorseful reverie. At the same time, a complex, difficult critique is aestheticized and thereby in some ways deflected, displaced or even nullified.

The smart bridge

Gone are the days when I worked on bridge design with a slide-rule, hand-operated mechanical calculator and bulky volumes of ten-figure logarithms. But the digital era has not just radically changed design, manufacture, logistics and project management, it has also been responsible for a revolution in the telling, promotion and selling of the bridge.

Extraordinary resources now exist online for anyone interested in anything about bridges, from engineering-oriented sites, both professional and corporate, to highly specific bridge blogs by fans, from educational sites to localized bridge heritage sites, from databases for posters, paintings and photos. This comparatively recent digitalizing of the telling, the way it has spawned a diversity of narrative genres around an immense compilation of bridge material and has made all this readily and quickly available, marks a dramatic moment in the story of the bridge.[75]

The extensive use of digitalization by creative advertising, especially around tourism and national or city branding, has profoundly extended the practice of 'selling' the bridge. As will be seen, the practice itself is certainly not new. In the USA, as early as the mid-nineteenth century, photographs of bridges on the new railways spreading westward were deliberately used to promote the railway line, the landscape, tourism and development of the 'frontier'.[76] But not only have crucial shifts occurred because of digital technology, such images of bridges are now embedded in a hyper-promotional culture, one in which boundaries of previously distinct genres are blurred and hybrid genres have emerged: infomercials, advergames, advertorials, infotainment. Under such a regime the bridge is both a commodity and a brand.

This shift between two orders of technology and their associated cultures, the one based on industrial construction that originated in the nineteenth century and the other based on digitalization, micro-electronics and virtual reality, is darkly explored in William Gibson's trilogy of cyber-punk novels set in the near future.[77] After a major earthquake damages the San Francisco–Oakland Bay Bridge, it is abandoned. Its transportation function is then superseded by a tunnel built using nanotechnology. A range of dispossessed people have illegally taken over the bridge. They are alienated or just excluded from the mainstream culture where inequalities of power and wealth have reached grotesque proportions and where fear and decadence run side by side. A vast squatter community, a shanty town full of vitality, emerges. A full range of technologies, both modern and postmodern, are used by the bridge community but in ways that are ad hoc and grassroot. This compares with the power- and wealth-driven use of advanced technology within corporations and organized crime. The massive decommissioned bridge is revealed as a complex and multifaceted series of places. It occupies an ambivalent position in the social structure. It is a site of fascination, one that is only just tolerated but also feared and even admired.

Approaching the bridge

What follows in this book are a series of in-depth examples that significantly develop the ideas sketched out in this introduction and thickly contextualize them. I have tried to avoid only focusing on the 'big' and the 'famous' bridges in these studies and instead have gone into detail about perhaps lesser known but no less significant examples. These include the ignored, or even invisible, bridges – often marginalized because they are deemed to be structurally mundane, or because their position lies outside the global spheres and networks dominated by a few wealthy and media-rich countries. The more famous bridges and contexts still receive their due attention. The hyper-contextualization or 'thick description' used in the case studies allows local, often marginalized, voices to speak, allows the complex and paradoxical nature of a bridge as a lived experience and as a site of contested imaginings to be explored.[78] Often the complexity of issues that entangle a bridge – whether its location, design, meanings, subsequent use, environmental or social impact, or artistic representation – cannot be understood without a careful elaboration of history and wider context. By triangulating out from these examples each chapter then fixes locations within a mapping of the bridge as 'a technology': of connection and separation; of the border; of reconciliation and estrangement; of mobility and immobility; of horizontality and verticality; of extension; of crossing; of nation- and city-building.

1 Technologies of Extension: Burt Creek to Lhasa

Burt Creek Bridge

About 50 kilometres north of Alice Springs, the unofficial capital city of Australia's desert centre, sits Burt Creek Bridge. A low, unprepossessing, reinforced concrete structure about 100 metres (330 ft) long, it carries the north–south intercontinental railway between the city of Adelaide – with its Mediterranean climate that characterizes the southern coast – through the aridity of Central Australia's semi-deserts to the tropical north and the city of Darwin.

Burt Creek is typical of the rivers of central Australia. A broad, untidy, sandy bed, lined by eucalyptus, it rarely carries any water, but is periodically subject to flash floods. Few travellers on the recently constructed transcontinental express would even know they were crossing Burt Creek Bridge. In many ways the bridges at Burt Creek, or over its tributary Ironbark Creek around 100 metres (330 ft) away, and at Harry Creek just a few kilometres closer to Alice Springs, are perhaps like hundreds of thousands of 'invisible', utilitarian bridges around the world that are vital to the circulation of rail and road traffic.

The construction of Burt Creek Bridge was integral to the 1,410-kilometre (875-mile) rail line that opened in 2004. This line completed a 2,720-kilometre north–south traverse of the Australian continent, work on which had originally begun around 100 years earlier. While the southern half of the line, from Adelaide in the south to Alice Springs at the continent's centre, was completed by 1929, the Alice Springs to Darwin half remained incomplete until a decision to go ahead in 2000. While most of the 97 bridges are similarly small and mostly invisible to passengers travelling on the line, there are six major ones over several large rivers in the tropical north, such as the Katherine, Adelaide and Elizabeth Rivers. A bridge 510 metres long, with pre-cast pre-stressed concrete girders and reinforced concrete deck, over the Elizabeth River, close to Darwin's port, is the longest on the new line.

Burt Creek Bridge, Northern Territory, Australia.

Almost 8,000 kilometres away, the route of the Qinghai–Tibet railway, the highest in the world, traces its way south from Golmud, the Xining capital of northwest China's Qinghai Province, and goes 1,142 kilometres to Lhasa. 960 kilometres of the track lies over 4,000 metres above sea level, with the highest point being 5,072 metres. Over 500 kilometres is laid in frozen earth. Work began in mid-2001 and was completed towards the end of 2006. Sumdar's bridge at Tanggulashan in the Tibetan Autonomous Region (TAR) of China is a relatively minor construction on this immense project. As part of their promotional-propaganda campaign the China–Tibet Information Centre celebrated Sumdar as 'an ordinary herder of the Tibetan ethnic group' who was looking forward to using the rail for a pilgrimage to Lhasa. He suggested a bridge be built at his home of Tanggulashan township because of his concern that the rail would 'block the access of herds to grazing lands'.[1] Sumdar, it is reported, 'invited construction officials and workers to the village . . . to celebrate the Spring Festival with the villagers' and told officials about his concerns and his solution. The result of this simple but perceptive request was a 32-metre bridge.

As with the Darwin–Alice Springs railway, the bridge at Tanggulashan is just one of hundreds of minor structures along the route. Also in common are several much larger bridges, as the rail crosses the Kunlun mountain pass at 4,767 metres and traverses several major rivers. The 11.7-kilometre Qingshui River Bridge is

The Elizabeth River Bridge, Northern Territory, Australia.

the longest of these, providing a frozen earth passage for wild animals following their traditional feeding and migration paths. The 2,276-metre long Doulung Large Bridge at the Yangbajain Canyon is built at an altitude of 4,150 metres. Other notable bridge constructions include the Kunlun Mountain Bridge, Tuotuo River Bridge, Sancha River Bridge, Beisangqu River Bridge and the Great Liuwu Bridge over the Kyichu River (the Lhasa River). In all, bridges make up 160 kilometres of the rail's length. The whole project been compared in magnitude to the Great Wall.

By linking up with the rail from Xining to Golmud, which had been completed earlier in 1984, the journey between Beijing and Lhasa can now be completed in just 48 hours, rather than taking many days of often difficult, and sometimes dangerous, travel by road.

The Kyichu (Lhasa) River Bridge (Liuwu Bridge).

The bridge as a technology of extension

This chapter addresses the place of bridges within vast systems of transportation, especially railways. In particular, the bridges at Burt Creek and Tanggulashan turn attention to the place of bridges, especially those of modest dimensions, within massively scaled projects of continental railway building in the twenty-first century. It has been over one hundred years since the end of the golden age of the construction of vast, nation-building, empire-consolidating, railway systems. Within such immense projects, the ability to design and quickly build efficient and reliable bridges, both big and small, was, and still is, crucial. What place do such railway projects now hold in an era of globalization, high-tech digitalized communication systems, cheap mass airline transportation, intercontinental highway systems and shipping containerization? What is the meaning of space–time *extension* in an era of space–time compression and global shrinkage?[2] How has the meaning of railway bridges changed along with the significance of the railway projects? Design and construction are now rarely the conspicuous display of the great designers. Both design and construction have been radically transformed over the past few decades by digitalization and globalization. Is there still a place for the heroics and idealism of 100 years ago?

Crossing tracks

Within such enormous transportation and communication systems, it is easy to overlook bridges, especially small or unspectacular ones, which are usually rendered almost invisible. They are seemingly overwhelmed by, and subservient to, the massive system itself. The unprepossessing structure at Burt Creek may be an extreme case, but even large bridges such as those over the Elizabeth River in northern Australia and the Lhasa River in Tibet can be relatively invisible. These bridges are smoothly, even seamlessly, incorporated into the railway system on a practical, aesthetic, cultural and political level. There is no pause or hesitation at the bridge, no change in tempo for the crossing. Even contemporary disciplines of social science, with their studies of communication and transportation, render these bridges invisible. They are incorporated into the rail or road and into the general notion of automobility or circulation, networks, and so on. There is a critical tension between the bridge as a unique moment, a site where a significant *crossing* occurs, and its relationship to an immensely extended *corridor* that comprises a complexity of technologies and places which are given coherence by the remorselessly uninterrupted rail tracks. Bridges, however, provide depth and verticality to horizontal extension.

The bridge is a technology for uninterrupted, unbroken, linear movement across any terrain. It establishes a hierarchy of tracks and achieves a sovereign right of way for the rail, while simultaneously creating safe passage for other tracks (rail, road, footpath, animal path, river, sacred route, and so on) that would otherwise be sliced through, blocked or severely disrupted by the rail. At the same time these 'other' tracks, no matter how important they may be to local culture, are usually rendered secondary, even subservient, to the rail and its corridor. The decision about where and how such crossings should occur, and which intersecting tracks should be blocked or left open, is not always just a practical matter, but one of power and imagination. The rail corridor is not just a vector going from A to B across a culturally empty landscape. It *always* imposes itself on a landscape that is criss-crossed by preexisting tracks, even in the cases of those, like Tibet, Australia and the USA, that traverse a vastness of so-called 'wilderness'. As will be seen, bridges as sites of a 'crossing over' are not only intersections between two or more different kinds of 'track', but often between two or more very different orders of imagination and of power around issues such as land, identity, mobility, community and sovereignty.

Of course, bridges are also used to 'overcome' natural obstacles, such as rivers and valleys. The locations of practical or even achievable crossings constrain the route totally. In the past, such possibilities were often limited by existing technology. The range of choice open to the contemporary engineer for sites of crossing has dramatically expanded with the revolution in materials, design and logistics that characterizes industrial society of the late twentieth and early twenty-first centuries. These bridge or crossing sites are not tightly focused nodes but constitute extensive *zones*. By having such defining power and influence over the route, the bridge creates a gathering of land, culture, mobility and imagination that extends outwards, both sideways from the rail line as well as for a considerable distance up and down the track. A bridge always creates a zone of disruption, disturbance and possibility.

The technology and politics of horizontality

Among systems of transportation, only a canal demands a more horizontal passage than does a railway. Schivelbusch reminds us that the railway, through an immense system of embankments, cuttings, tunnels and bridges, introduced a virtually horizontal, extended traverse of countryside and town, with the train a mobile viewing platform.[3] Such horizontality led to the development of the panorama as a 'new', or at least dominant, form of perception. There is something imperious and detached about the panoramic gaze. The remorseless horizontality also dovetailed with the requirements of bridges which, despite a sometimes pronounced upward curve over its span, are nearly always built as close to the horizontal as possible. To this extent the bridge is itself a technology of horizontality, while at the same time creating a moment of complexity, depth and verticality to simple linear, horizontal extension. The requirement of horizontality has a profound effect on the railway route and, hence, on the positioning of bridges.

The bridges on the Tibetan and Australian railway projects are vital components in the extension of power – economic, political and social – in an age of global shrinkage and high-tech communications. Previous comparable rail systems were built, mostly during the nineteenth century, at times of unprecedented and generally brutal expansion and consolidation of power, by an aggressive and triumphant capitalism that treated the labour force harshly and the colonized and displaced peoples around the globe even worse. These immense projects were involved in the creation of new concepts of time and space, concepts that generally celebrated expansion and global connection, whilst at the same time generating concerns about excessive speed and loss of traditional values.[4] The new milieu valued collective regularity and discipline where time was concerned but prompted fears about a loss of individuality and spontaneity.

While the Australian and Chinese rail projects share similarities in their relation to economic development, nation building, military concerns, regionalism, resource extraction, settlement and tourism, there are profound differences in their approach to issues of power, colonialism and post-colonialism and indigenous-rights issues. As we shall see, while both projects have received acclaim they have also been criticized for their economic, social, environmental and cultural impacts.

The template for these long-distance rail and bridge networks in Australia and Tibet/China was laid early in the nineteenth century. The archetype was the extraordinary system of British rail and bridge construction which was not only the world's first but which was subsequently extended throughout the British Empire, particularly in India and Africa.[5] The British were quickly joined by the USA which created perhaps the first truly *extensive*, transcontinental network of rail and bridges. From Siberia to Canada, the nineteenth century saw the construction of massive networks of rail, tunnels and bridges for which the conquest of immense distance and of 'untamed' but resource-rich 'wilderness' was the goal and nation-building the project. These founding projects all paid scant regard to the 'local'. Local issues, along with those of the environment and of working conditions, were considered to be insignificant as compared with the grand design and imperative of national greatness, unlimited commercial growth, and technologically-driven social improvement. Nevertheless, within such a ruthless climate, extraordinary experiments and advances in bridge design and construction occurred. In addition, these bridges became icons of a new identity and focal points for the complex and contentious debates that accompanied this revolution.

Bridges and the nineteenth-century rail networks: Britain

The canal era, from the mid-eighteenth century onwards, both in the scale of construction and the demand for exact horizontality, saw a steady increase in the construction of bridges throughout Britain. New techniques of construction and design as well as modifications to older, tried and tested ones, were gradually developed. The industrial age of bridges with its new materials, new design and, importantly, its new social and industrial relationships for manufacture and construction was ushered in with the completion in 1779 of Iron Bridge at Coalbrookedale in England. It also initiated an age of experimentation in bridge design.

However, the birth of the railway era, from the 1830s onwards, brought about an unprecedented expansion in the demand for bridges whose numbers soared in direct relation to the extraordinary growth in track laying. Britain was the pioneer in railway construction, with over 11,000 kilometres of track criss-crossing the country by 1850. But the sheer mileage of rail track was not the only factor demanding a corresponding expansion of bridge construction. The two unique properties of railways, following on from canals and in contrast to roads, were their insistence on horizontality and on large radius curves when changing direction. Both of these characteristics placed severe constraints on possible routes and thereby demanded an unparalleled modification of landscape through the construction of cuttings, tunnels, embankments and, most spectacularly, vast numbers of bridges. Such a surge in demand for bridges and the economic requirements for speedy project completion not only provoked experimentation in materials and design but in an industrial form of production, manufacture and construction. Just as significant was the requirement for these bridges to withstand, for the very first time in history, an industrial scale of loading. The weight and momentum, the sustained violence caused by the vibration of a railway engine and carriages passing, repeatedly, over a bridge at an unheard of velocity, was of an entirely new order for bridges.

In addition, the inbuilt logic of this new industrial form of capitalism compelled a constant revolutionizing of railway technology. This was aided by the parallel revolution in communication technology engendered by telegraph and telegraph-controlled signalling. These in turn permitted a dramatic increase in scale and complexity of railway operations on any given track. Hence the size, power, speed and number of trains passing over these bridges were constantly increasing in the early decades of the railway era, levelling off only towards the end of the century as steam and telegraph technologies reached their limits. While these demands were felt most strongly by, and were most dramatically visible in, the ingenious designs of large constructions such as the Britannia Railway Bridge of 1838, the countless numbers of smaller bridges were no less subject to the testing new regime. Older materials, such as wood, brick or stone, and designs, such as the classic arch, were modified to cope. An additional, unexpected factor also quickly emerged: industrial pollution. This had a deleterious effect on the strength and durability of construction materials. This in turn created an entirely new order, scale and hence cost of bridge maintenance alongside that of track maintenance, one which constantly lagged well behind demand. The consequence of this inability or unwillingness to adequately maintain existing bridges is still felt today. While major bridges, such as over Sydney Harbour or the Firth of Forth, receive constant care and maintenance, thousands of bridges around the world are in a state of dangerous disrepair.

The calculated loading on a railway bridge designed and built in 1840 was obsolete only a decade later. What protected most bridges from severe damage or collapse was their excessive redundancy in design and construction. This was partly due to the infancy of engineering mathematics, and miscalculations in the strength and behaviour of key structural material. To compensate for these uncertainties engineers would overdesign in critical areas just to be on the safe side. In other words, the over-design of bridges saved most of them. While engineers drew on past experience where possible, the new materials and performance requirements for bridges pushed them into completely new territory. Over-confidence, bad luck, poor judgement, inferior quality materials and construction – allied with dubious business and manufacturing practices, poor management and supervision, plus the dictates of cost-cutting to enhance profits – resulted in numerous bridge-related accidents, many small (albeit often serious for those concerned), and quite a few disastrously spectacular.

Bridges provided a focus, condensing both the triumph and terror of the new mechanical technology and the horror and exhilaration of speed. This was the era of great heroic constructions and the new breed of designer-builders, the new 'engineers' such as Thomas Telford, John Rennie, John Roebling, Robert Stephenson and Isambard Kingdom Brunel, became household names. The expansion of newspapers with their exploitation of the new techniques of visual reproduction facilitated a widespread distribution of dramatic lithographs of catastrophic accidents, such as that which befell the Tay Bridge in Scotland on a stormy December night in 1879. The Tay Bridge collapse, a major blow to Victorian Britain's industrial pride, produced a doubling of the horror – a complete train was lost as well as a considerable section of the bridge.

The dramatic appearance in, and transformation of, the rural environment and landscape was greeted with both concern and celebration. Landscape paintings that tried to record or interpret the new rail and its bridges in rural Britain were few. Older bridges were the popular subject of painters of the picturesque and, later, of the Romantic sublime. Photography, still in its infancy, fulfilled the role of documenting the new, industrial design bridges. Turner's 1844 *Rain, Steam and Speed* was an exception to the rule, with its portrayal, interpretation and celebration of a modern rail bridge.

In a comprehensive analysis Stephen Daniels argues that Turner's painting is not just a representation of a railway or a bridge, but a transcontinental corridor. The railway in question is the Great

Western. As Daniels points out, 'Brunel conceived the Great Western as an extensive enterprise, stretching from Britain to the United States'.[6] This rail company, the nation's largest and most glamorous at the time, went from London to Bristol, one of the major ports for the transatlantic crossing to America. Brunel, the central figure of the railway, being its chief designer and engineer, also designed the radically new steamship, appropriately named the *Great Western*, based in Bristol. Turner was himself a shareholder in the rail company. Daniels points to these founding railway companies as representatives of a 'new political-economic order'.[7] At the time the 'levelling of railway track' was frequently used as a 'metaphor for the levelling of class distinctions'.[8] With rail construction and expansion often opposed by the established landed gentry, many of these were brought onside, objections muted, by

J.M.W. Turner, *Rain, Steam, and Speed – The Great Western Railway*, 1844, oil on canvas.

becoming shareholders in the new railway companies. Representations of these bridges were used as promotional devices to 'sell' the projects as a whole.

Turner's bridge painting not only frames, focuses and condenses these issues, it also reveals a crossing replete with additional complex symbolism. The painting exposes a conjunction of major routes, showing the river as no mere obstacle to be crossed. The river is the Thames, an icon of established British identity, commercial and State power and an earlier mode of transportation. The crossing of this river thereby signals the eclipse of the old order and the start of something new. The presence of the old road bridge reinforces this sense of a past being left behind. The new structure is the Maidenhead Bridge, completed in 1839. With 92 metres of river to be spanned as cleanly as possible, Brunel used two semi-

Maidenhead Bridge on the River Thames, linking Berkshire and Buckinghamshire.

elliptical arches that, at the time, were the longest yet built. Importantly, Maidenhead Bridge was a site of complex controversies and disputes – engineering, financial and social. There were dire predictions of its imminent collapse. Daniels suggests that the painting is a play on both promotional and critical material of the time, with Turner consciously using similar devices. Daniels carefully unpacks the interlocking of rail, bridge, Thames and London within a burgeoning ideology of global and national 'circulation' and a struggle for political reform within Britain.[9]

The spectacular bridges began to function as icons of this new vision of nation-state and commerce-society. While such a triumphant perspective was sometimes celebrated, albeit ambivalently, via the large new bridges outside London, as in Turner's painting, the symbolic fulcrum of this changing vision lay in the capital itself. With London emerging as the world's premier cosmopolitan metropolis it was the city's core, gathered around the bridges over the Thames, that provided the main focus for this radical shift in sensibility. In Dickens's mid-century novel *Little Dorrit*, the story constantly circulates across London and Southwark Bridges, completed in 1831 and 1819 respectively. While London Bridge is portrayed as a busy thoroughfare, the iron bridge at Southwark provides a space of hope and reverie. At this time London had become the world's greatest imperial port, the centre of the world's most extensive railway system. The City was the world's leading financial centre. New dimensions of mobility, social organization and the regulation of time came to be embodied in the City of London. The Thames bridges were not only integral to this new identity but technologies for its realization. Herman Melville, in his 1855 novel *Israel Potter*, celebrated the extraordinary human flow over London Bridge, which, while it had been going on for centuries, was now of an entirely new intensity, 'the greatest everyday crowd which grimy

London presents to the curious stranger'.[10] London's grime, like the ceaseless flow of humanity over its bridges, was evidence of unprecedented industry and energy.

The number of bridges being built through the nineteenth century, not only in Britain but around the world, was unparalleled. Most other European countries quickly began to construct their national railway systems.[11] The engineering solutions being explored to carry the railways across daunting natural obstacles were extraordinarily diverse. For example, the Goltzsch Valley Bridge in Saxony, opened in 1851, was 78 metres high and 574 metres long. Constructed of granite and brick, it had a massive and imposing presence. By contrast, the 1877 Maria Pia Bridge in Portugal, built by the French engineer Gustave Eiffel, utilized his radical ideas about open lattice steel construction to span 160 metres. Eiffel went on to design the even longer Garabit Viaduct (162 metres) in France, which was completed in 1884. These bridges, both great and small, were crucial technologies for completely new experiences of time and space. Bridges such as Maidenhead were integral to the Great Western Railway's capacity to cut the time of a journey from London and Bristol to just five hours (compared to somewhere between 24 and 48 hours by horse-drawn coach over extremely poor roads). The other crucial development was a new unprecedented reliability and consistency of land travel, built around a complex network of timetables.

Bridges and the nineteenth-century rail networks

In the second half of the nineteenth century the railways became a major technology of imperial expansion and colonization, with the British as the dominant industrial and imperial power at the time, again leading the way. India had its first railway as early as 1853; however, further development was slow but steady. By 1870

there were nearly 2,000 kilometres of track and just ten years later this had grown to 14,500 kilometres. The imperatives of bridge design in a vast country lacking industrial capacity were economy and functionality. Experimentation was low on the agenda. In Africa the rail had an additional visionary quality, driven as it was by a charismatic and ruthless individual for whom personal profit and national glory formed a devastating partnership. While the Cape to Cairo vision of Cecil Rhodes was only one aspect of extensive programme of rail construction across Africa, it somehow encapsulated the politics of an extension in its pure form – a mix of profit, conquest, exploitation and extraordinary engineering across a vast 'wilderness'.[12] The bridge that symbolized all these complex and contradictory dimensions was probably the one over the Zambesi River at Victoria Falls. Here was the world's largest waterfall, a huge ravine that provided a natural challenge and spectacular display for British engineering and social superiority. Completed between 1903 and

Garabit Viaduct, Massif Central, France, completed 1884.

1905, the Zambesi Bridge, with its steel arch spanning 156.5 metres, carrying both rail and road traffic 128 metres above the base of the falls, imposed itself precisely at the most visually dramatic point. A dubious environmental and aesthetic intrusion by today's standards, the bridge asserted British and European power and encapsulated a heady mix of idealism and greed.[13]

Railway construction in the USA followed quickly on the British lead. Confined initially to the eastern seaboard, it was well established by the 1840s. There was a dramatic surge in rail building from the 1840s to the outbreak of the Civil War in 1861. Not only were complex networks established along the eastern seaboard, rail tracks were extended westward into the interior and to the points from which wagons set off, taking settlers and adventurers to the far west of the continent. This 'manifest destiny', the expansion westward and inclusion of all continental North America into a single national entity, was really just another name for a colonial and imperial adventure, no different in kind – with its mix of idealism, greed, sense of national identity and engineering achievement – from the Russians in Siberia or the British in Africa. But it set in motion what was to become the archetype of a political technology of extension: the transcontinental railway.

In the mid-nineteenth century railroads were idealized as a symbol of American capitalism's capacity for dynamic growth. While the overall railway 'system' was the prime focus of acclaim (and some condemnation), bridge building provided the most concentrated visual focus. The bridges ranged from quickly assembled timber truss structures to immense steel spans that single-handedly challenged not only the limits of the spanning capacity of the time but were themselves triumphant testaments to an aggressively expansionist American modernity.

Rail brought about a revolution in bridge design. By 1850 a whole range of new bridge designs were appearing, many in timber. But massive moving loads had to be carried. The increase in rail traffic made it clear that iron and wood truss bridges generally lacked adequate strength. The onset of sudden vibrations proved too much for many bridges and there were numerous collapses. Then, in 1847, *A Work on Bridge Building* appeared, its author, Squire Whipple, a self-taught engineer from New York. Whipple's book is recognized as

The World's Highest Single Pile Trestle, USA, 1913.

the 'first American attempt to supply a theoretical means for calculating stress in truss bridges instead of the rule of thumb methods employed until that time, [and it] marked the emergence of a scientific approach to bridge building'.[14] The Whipple Bowstring Truss Bridge was a great success and many copied this approach.

The precise nature of what a bridge actually crosses is always of great significance to the meanings circulating through the structure. So, when the iconic Mississippi River finally needed to be bridged in order to let the city of St Louis challenge the rail-driven ascendancy of Chicago, it was a major event, both practical and symbolic. This crossing was itself a testament to the rise of the railroad and the diminishing importance of the river in terms of communication and transportation. By 1860 Chicago had benefited dramatically from its position as a hub for numerous rail lines, while the very river that had been St Louis's advantage was becoming a hindrance, an obsta-

Whipple cast and wrought iron bowstring truss bridge of 1867, Albany, New York state.

cle that isolated the city from the nation's westward expansion. James Eads's bridge was built between 1867 and 1874.[15] Celebrated by Walt Whitman, the three arch spans made a bridge that was longer and higher than any other in the USA, and it was the first time steel had been used on such a large bridge. Economically, however, it was a failure, being underused and over budget.

Niagara Falls had earlier presented an opportunity to bridge an iconic natural feature, one that would also provide the designer with a spectacular engineering challenge. Given the successful designer was the philosophically-inclined John Roebling, eventually of Brooklyn Bridge fame, the Niagara Falls crossing was also a display of transcendental spiritualism. Born in Germany in 1806, he became a student and friend of Hegel. For Roebling, mathematics was equivalent to pure spiritual perception and the suspension bridge was the manifestation of a spiritual ideal. Whilst in Germany he published underground radical papers which explored the idea

Eads Bridge over the Mississippi River at St Louis, Missouri, photographed in 1983.

of mastering nature and soaring to freedom. Roebling wrote extensively on the topic of spiritualism, including comments on the works of Swedenborg and Emerson. He was involved in séances and automatic writing. He wrote that 'spiritualising nature is the aim and end of creation'.[16] The dramatic waterfalls were ideally suited to Roebling's vision, providing the perfect setting for a display of human achievement in spiritualizing nature.

Functionally, the Niagara suspension bridge was a crucial link in the connection of New York with the expanding Midwest cities. But, as Danly points out, it was also one 'of the first bridges to attract the attention of photographers'.[17] The bridge, completed in 1855, quickly became a tourist attraction in its own right and a promotional icon for the railway. Daguerreotypes and stereoscopic views were readily available as early as 1856.

This early combination of photography with bridge engineering was crucial and also directly affected the way painting represented

Niagara Falls Suspension Bridge, hand-coloured lithograph, c. 1856.

bridges. The documentary style that dominated early photography seemed to suit a vision of technological achievement. It offered a mix of grainy detail and spectacular views. On the other hand, three mid-nineteenth century paintings reveal the complex struggle taking place in America about how to understand the sudden presence of this new industrial technology in the landscape.

The Starrucca Viaduct, completed in 1848 with a length of 317 metres, was one of the few masonry rail bridges to be built in America in the first half of the nineteenth century. The nation and the railway companies were both in a hurry and stone bridges were generally just too costly and too slow to build. The viaduct was the most famous bridge on the New York and Erie Railroad and was labelled the 'Eighth Wonder of the World' by its admirers, a common appellation for a number of bridges of that era. With its multiple high arches, it harked back to pre-modern forms, even, for some admirers, echoing the architecture of ancient Rome. The incorpora-

Niagara Falls Suspension Bridge, promotional print for the railway, c. 1876.

tion of concrete in the footings was one of first uses of this material in the USA. It was also the most expensive railway bridge built up to that time. Jasper Francis Cropsey's 1865 painting *Starrucca Viaduct, Pennsylvania* shows a train passing across the viaduct located in the middle distance. It is embedded within a 'wilderness' landscape of mountains, forests and calm water, with languid figures in the foreground viewing the scene, classically framed by a few trees. As Susan Danly suggests, the 'railroad thus appears in an idealized setting, suggesting the easy assimilation of new technological forms into the aesthetic mode of the picturesque'.[18] There is no celebration of a technological sublime.

By contrast with this unproblematic representation of rail and bridge, George Inness's famous 1855 painting, *The Lackawanna Valley*, with its stark depiction of a profound intrusion of the new technology into the landscape, reveals a deep moral ambivalence towards material progress and its impact on land and culture. As

Jaspar Francis Cropsey, *Starrucca Viaduct, Pennsylvania*, 1865, oil on canvas.

Leo Marx points out, the painting, with a small, almost invisible, bridge at its centre, shows not just a new technology but a new 'technological system', one of the first representations of 'the new machine technology as a determinant and a visible emblem of a new kind of large-scale, expansionary, corporate enterprise'.[19]

The construction of the 2,865-kilometre transcontinental railway linking the Atlantic and Pacific coasts took only four years, being completed in 1869. While there were other lines that followed in traversing the continent, it was this original venture that fired the imagination. Bridges functioned as symbols of the joining of east and west coasts. Walt Whitman celebrated the railway 'as part of a global system which included the Atlantic and Pacific cable and the Suez canal'.[20] Its numerous bridges not only provided the crucial crossing technologies, their visual representations were used to sell the project and to provide it with an aesthetic legitimation. This was because bridges were one of the few, if not only, truly complex and monumental structures along the line. For example, Andrew Joseph Russell, in his album, *The Great West Illustrated* of 1869, 'used bridge structures to organize panoramic landscapes'.[21] While the album stressed the West as an untamed wilderness ready to be economically exploited, it also played multiple other roles – documenting and publicizing the rail, 'educating the public in the geography and geology of the West, advertising the scenic attractions along the route, and providing aesthetic images of the western landscape'.[22] As Daniels points out, however, the pioneering and agricultural opportunities being promoted were framed by a remorseless expansion of 'corporate organization and machine technology'.[23] The transcontinental railway provoked confrontation between white settlers and Native Americans with catastrophic impacts on indigenous life and culture, as well as on native fauna and flora.[24]

The West featured prominently from the very beginning of American cinema and many films depicted the building of the transcontinental railway lines. However, bridges seldom made an appearance in westerns.[25] Perhaps bridge construction was too slow for the required pace of movies about the westward expansion. Certainly, bridge construction was hardly mentioned in these films, except as site of catastrophe. One exception that provided a retrospective reflection was *Pillars of the Sky* (1956) which portrays the impact of a bridge on Native Americans and their land.[26] The bridge was supposedly built by the US army in 1868 in Oregon county and spanned a river with the aim of taking a road across the reservation. But, the tribal chiefs considered its construction to be a treaty violation and became determined to fight against it.

The rail-bridge to Lhasa

Two contemporary rail projects and their associated bridges, in Australia and Tibet, resonate against the template laid down in the golden era of transcontinental railways discussed above. Virtually every issue and every idealistic vision that surfaced over 100 years ago has its counterpart in these two modern projects. But, as will be seen, it would be a mistake to see them merely as variations on an old theme. In order fully to appreciate the complex place of the bridges within these schemes it is necessary to develop a fairly detailed overview of each one.

The contemporary rail construction in Tibet occurs at a time of China's rise as a superpower, anxious to consolidate economic expansion and to assert territorial integrity. Many problems and issues confronted the construction of the Qinghai–Tibet railway and its bridges, not least the extreme conditions to be encountered in its surroundings: the remoteness of the construction from any

major industrial and supply centres; the high altitude and thereby
lack of oxygen for the construction workers; the plummeting tem-
peratures in winter. Unlike similar constructions on the Trans-
Siberian and Canadian Pacific railways, the one in Tibet had to
traverse long sections not just of frozen earth, but of frozen earth
rendered unstable by seasonal temperature fluctuations – high
levels of sunshine and a relatively high earth temperature. To cope
with this temperature variation and with an expected global warming which will make the ground even more unstable, a unique,
albeit expensive, bridge-style railroad was devised. Considerable
sections of the railroad are in fact carried over 'invisible' bridges.
These extraordinary bridges take the rail across potentially unstable ground by means of foundation supports that go deep down
to rest directly on the permafrost. In such sections, the ground
above the permafrost has little structural significance. The convention that bridges should have a visible gap beneath their span is
irrelevant. In this project, therefore, bridges are not just essential

The Qinghai–Tibet railway.

connecting links, comparatively small in length given the scale of the railway, but critical in function. In sheer length alone the visible or conventional bridges – well over 600 according to some estimates – make up a significant proportion of the 'rail', around 7 per cent. When the invisible 'rail-bridges' are added it becomes clear that the bridges are not just more intimately involved in the rail project than is usual but are also *extensively* a part of it.

Many concerns were expressed about the environmental impact of such a massive project. Already, global warming is melting the permafrost on which the track and bridges have been built. Unexpected sinking and cracking of the bridges has occurred, rendering the rail unstable in some places.[27] The railway also traverses Hoh Xil, a wildlife zone used by migrating animals. To allow for this, a bridge-like safety channel acts as a passage for animals under the railway. Yet some have insisted that these much-publicized environmentally-friendly bridges are in fact a major hazard, even death traps. Apparently, sheep, yaks, Tibetan antelopes (chiru) and wild ass (kyang) do not wander through in ones and twos but rush under the bridges in huge packs and the gaps between the pillars are too small to accommodate this. There are claims that scores of young and weak animals are dying in stampedes.[28]

While the Qinghai–Tibet Railway has been described in the publication *China Today* as an 'Engineering Miracle',[29] opponents of the project have called it a railway built on lies and deceit, expressing misgivings about whether the railway has ensured the well-being, and even survival, of the Tibetan people in their own land or signalled an approaching doom for Tibetan culture.[30] To say that Beijing's view of Tibet, and of the railway, differs from that commonly held in the west, or by exiled Tibetans, would be a gross understatement.

For many mainland Chinese, Tibet occupies a paradoxical position, somewhat akin to the frontier in US national fantasies of the nineteenth century. While for some it has deep spiritual and religious connotations, for many others, especially the government in Beijing and Lhasa, it is a legitimate region to defend, explore, exploit and develop. A short-term El Dorado for many seeking their fortune, it is perceived to be a place of exoticism, spirituality and colour, but also of dirty, potentially violent and superstitious nomads and resentful locals.[31]

The US–Tibet Committee critique of the railway project was typical of an overwhelming condemnation from groups in western countries that were trying to stop its construction: 'This is a politically motivated project. China is building this railway to consolidate its military and economic control over occupied Tibet . . . The Tibet railway is among the greatest current threats to Tibet's survival.'[32] Environmental threats listed include increased mineral extraction, damage to wildlife, contamination of significant water bodies and inducement of soil erosion.

Numerous western-based Tibetan activist groups insist that the project will enormously enhance China's military capacity throughout the Tibetan plateau, increase the threat to India's security and provide even more momentum to China's nuclear programme in the region. The Beijing government has been accused of designing the railway 'to facilitate increased Chinese population transfer and economic migration into Tibet, further diluting the Tibetan population and threatening Tibet's cultural survival.'[33] Exiled Tibetans have been unequivocal in their concerns and condemnations.[34]

The issue of development in Tibet is a contentious one for western supporters of the Tibetan cause and can be oversimplified by sharply juxtaposing an idyllic traditional culture, frozen in time and virtually untouched by modernity, with a brutally modernized, industrial landscape of concrete, pollution and collapsing social values. It is difficult to separate engineering achievement from social impact.[35] Tenzin Dargyal, president of the Canada Tibet Committee, commented that, as 'a Tibetan and a Quebecer . . . I support development in Tibet, but not development that is imposed by Beijing and principally serves the interests of the Chinese Communist Party, rather than the great majority of Tibetans'.[36]

The extensive destruction of traditional Tibetan housing and villages, plus the resettlement of Tibetan communities, has long been a disturbing feature of Chinese governance throughout Tibet. The construction of the Lhasa Station precipitated the demolition of the village of Ne'u and the resettlement of its inhabitants. This action has been criticized as being without justification on a purely practical level. Once again, the more conventionally recognizable bridges provide a sharp focus for both celebration and critique. The Liuwu Bridge over the Kyichu (Lhasa) River is integral to the functioning of Lhasa Station, connecting it with central Lhasa on the opposite bank.

The railway construction drew thousands of Chinese labourers, with complaints that few jobs existed for Tibetans during construction, or would even be created for Tibetans once railway operations commenced. It was reported, for example, that of 500 people working on the construction of the 929-metre Liuwu Bridge (Lhasa River Bridge), 'only a tiny number was found to be Tibetan'.[37] An incredulous Agence France-Presse correspondent, noting the large numbers of Chinese who were sweeping and pushing wheelbarrows, was told by the chief engineer that Tibetans 'don't have the technical training needed for the task'.[38] The Liuwu Bridge has also been blamed for water contamination: 'The once potable water of the Lhasa River is now so polluted as to be unfit for drinking.'[39]

As would be expected, official Chinese pronouncements labelled such concerns as absurd: 'The local people in Tibet generally are

New buildings in the Ne'u area, Tibet.

Construction of the Kyichu (Lhasa) Bridge, Tibet.

eagerly awaiting its opening. Devout Buddhists expect to make pilgrimage to Wutai Mountain after the opening; common people expect to tour and visit inland areas by rail; and more people hope the railway can bring along more convenient materials and more affluent life.'[40] Fears of the 'Han-ization' of Tibet are dismissed, while headlines proclaim Tibetan celebrations. With extensive use of their images on the official websites, the bridges provide stunning visual confirmation of the achievement, encapsulating Beijing's celebration of the technical triumph and heroics of the railway as a whole. As with all such extensive rail projects it is extremely difficult to capture the grandeur with simple images of railway tracks. Criticism of the rail is deflected or even effaced by the aesthetic power of its bridges.

The rail is part of an ambitious plan to develop China's 'West' with Lhasa imagined within a fantasy of futuristic modernity that seems to echo, at least in terms of representational genre, the vision of 1950s USA with its sleek bridges and complex freeway intersections. Development continues to be seen by Beijing as the key to stability in the region.[41]

While traditional culture is disappearing, faux-Tibetan aesthetics are being incorporated as iconic gestures in the new architecture of the railway. The design of Lhasa Station with its inward-sloping walls mimics one of the classic features of Tibetan architecture but expresses this in a rigidly monumental regularity that is alien to traditional Tibet. This cultural appropriation is also seen in posters celebrating the railway that showcase the Potala Palace. This was the home of the Dalai Lama, now in exile, and is one of traditional Tibet's most revered buildings. A key image of hope and resistance for many Tibetans, it has been turned into a themed museum. The struggle over the Potala encapsulates the war of signs and images taking place around the railway and its bridges.[42]

Officials in the Tibetan Autonomous Region have celebrated the rail and compared its impact with the railway's contribution to the opening up of the American West.[43] However, for some Americans this reference carries a dark shadow and the US–Tibet Committee's warning contained a reminder about the millions of Native Americans killed and marginalized in the process of this railroad expansion.[44] Others have compared Chinese soldiers slaughtering animals for hides in Tibet with the parallels in western history.[45]

Many in western countries are still concerned about the impact of past rail and bridge construction in the oppression of the local and indigenous peoples and, understandably, are sensitized towards any contemporary repetitions.

Billboard showing forthcoming development in Lhasa – the Liuwu Bridge and ring road that will connect the two banks of the Kyichu River.

Intersecting tracks: Bridges from Alice Springs to Darwin

As with the new rail bridges in Tibet, those in Australia encapsulate, intensify, deflect and aestheticize the complexes that circulate through the total rail project. The new continental rail system in Australia, like its Chinese counterpart in Tibet, cannot help but be directly and intimately involved with indigenous culture, and as a corollary, with issues of power, identity, imagination and control. In both cases, questions about national identity and nation building

Billboard in Lhasa depicting the Potala Palace. The Chinese text reads 'Disseminate the good news about the Quinghai–Tibet railway and Lhasa will spring anew'.

Billboard of Lhasa Station.

inevitably focus on a struggle between dominant cultures and alternative, marginalized visions of nation and identity.

The bridges on these projects provide lenses into various realignments in global politics, economics and space–time engendered by the new techno-cultures of mobility and communication. Both cases, too, are haunted by historical injustice and oppression, particularly in terms of indigenous cultures, by a relative failure of a development process driven by a techno-triumphalist ideology. In 1928 rail construction in Australia's tropical north, around Katherine, employed about 500 white men. They reportedly 'left behind alcohol, venereal disease, and part-coloured children'.[46] Oppressive actions and gross ignorance generally accompanied all earlier rail construction.[47]

Unlike Tibet, where religion and local culture always defer to socialism and national economic development, the situation in contemporary Australia, though far from perfect, is very different. There is a measure of sensitivity towards indigenous issues, particularly religion. While, as will be seen in the discussion of the Hindmarsh Island Bridge in Chapter Three, many people are upset and frustrated by indigenous demands, a respect for Aboriginal heritage sites and land ownership is both a legal requirement and, for many, an essential aspect of a widespread, albeit fraught, renegotiation and re-imagining of national identity and purpose.

As discussed above, markers of traditional Tibetan culture have been incorporated into the promotional rhetoric that circulates through the bridges and rail system in the TAR or Chinese occupied Tibet. Similarly, Australia has, in recent decades, increasingly advertised itself with images of Aboriginality. Some of the engines pulling the passenger coaches on the transcontinental lines have been decorated with Aboriginal-inspired dot paintings.

The construction of Burt and Harry Creek bridges and the longer ones over the Elizabeth and Katherine rivers occurred within a context in which non-indigenous culture is disturbed by guilt, shame and uncertainty, plus a widespread desire for healing and rapprochement. At the same time mainstream Australia, as a nation, is involved in a crucial process of global realignment – away from Britain and towards the Asia-Pacific. Opportunities and anxieties have been aroused, from concerns about military defence and border protection (about political and economic refugees and asylum seekers, terrorism, illegal fishing and drug smuggling from the north) to excitement about possibilities for trade and tourism, with Darwin the doorway to Asia.

The proposed railway cuts through complex debates about Australian identity, with the bridges becoming focal points that sharply concentrate, in an intensely practical way, many of the issues. As the indigenous Northern Land Council has emphasized, nearly all the 1,414 kilometres of land being traversed by the railway is Aboriginal. Each bridge location along the line is therefore potentially a site of an intense renegotiation of Australian settlement, a struggle over radically different views of the world.[48]

The relationship between local indigenous people and the new railway is complex. While it has been acknowledged that substantial training and employment opportunities have occurred in some regions, elsewhere the promised jobs have not eventuated. Even so, locomotives involved in the construction were ceremoniously given Aboriginal names chosen by local Aboriginal leaders. Traditional dancers welcomed the construction trains to their town. Attention was given to indigenous cultural issues and rights during the planning, surveying and construction phases, even if decisions were often contentious. There were many negotiations over the railway's intersection with all types of existing tracks. Burt Creek Bridge, for example, is the site of an intense, complex and contentious series of crossings.

Bridges are often the site of intensely local negotiations, struggles and bargaining, the importance of which is frequently belied by the apparent material insignificance of the place as compared with the immensity of the overall project. While many local concerns about community, safety, access and environment are common to all groups across Australia, at times the local beliefs are totally at variance to those of the western post-Enlightenment science, technology and development world view that drives the railway and bridge construction. At Burt Creek, decisions about where to locate the bridge site had to take into account a whole range of other 'crossings' – sacred dreaming tracks, those of everyday life in the local indigenous communities, those associated with various fauna and flora. An impact study reported the following:

> The Burt Creek area not only hosts a well-established outstation, but also dangerous sites associated with mpwere (maggots) and amenge (blow fly) Dreamings. If the mulga trees, which are understood to be the amenge (blow flies), are disturbed maggots will rise from the ground and infest the genitalia of train passengers and anyone else who ventured near the damaged trees. The concerns of the custodians of these sites have been consistent over a long period of consultation about the railway and work restrictions have been put in place as a condition of approval of construction in this area. The concerns that custodians have about protection of particular trees in this area require that these trees be identified and fully protected during construction.[49]

Many field inspections and consultations were undertaken. The impact report emphasized that it 'is essential that work restrictions aimed at preserving the integrity of these sites is adhered to during construction activities'.[50] It was insisted that construction crews must be accompanied by a team of appropriate custodians and

traditional owners were adamant about construction workers receiving localized cross-cultural training.

Concerns were expressed about the noise of trains and the effects of vibration on the water bore and tin sheds that constituted the settlement at Burt Creek.[51] There was a need to ensure an adequate passage for hunting and for visiting important sites. A short distance away, at Harry Creek, another bridge site close to another indigenous community, there were similar worries about noise, safety and access. This was an already disrupted community in need of healing. Apprehension was voiced about wildlife management and about the disturbance of a nearby family cemetery.[52]

Over 1,000 kilometres to the north of Burt Creek the railway has to cross the large, tropical Katherine River. Known to the local indigenous Jawoyn people as Nitmiluk, the Katherine River and gorge are not only crucial tourist spots for the region's economy,

Burt Creek Bridge, Northern Territory, Australia.

they have been described as being central 'to the process of an indigenous (re)construction of post-colonial space', to the project of reclaiming and reinscribing 'Aboriginal spatial identities after colonial experiences of appropriation and contempt'.[53] The rail project therefore inevitably became enmeshed in issues around employment and training opportunities, land tenure, and the role of symbolism and cultural art.

Part of rebuilding the Jawoyn Nation involves inscribing space with indigenous meanings. The Jawoyn Association therefore recommended that 'traditional owners and native title holders be acknowledged as having a right to name places along the entire rail route'.[54] To this extent, for example, attention had to be given to 'culturally significant paperbark trees in the vicinity of the railway crossing over Coomalie Creek'.[55] This may seem a small detail from the perspective of a multi-million dollar, 2,720-kilometre national project, but, like many other such details, it highlights the requirement for a mutual sensitivity at a crossing between two totally different conceptions of development, progress, place and identity. For example, closer to Darwin the railway crosses the wide Elizabeth River. The main structural problem facing the long Elizabeth Bridge at this tropical location lay with the possibility of corrosion of the tubular steel piles due to the tropical marine environment. The Elizabeth River Bridge, completed at the very end of 2002, had to satisfy indigenous concerns about access and maintaining tracks used for fishing trips to the Elizabeth River and to the harbour area. Contemporary promotion of the completed bridge, of course, effaces all such complexities as it would any labour disputes, design or construction problems, focusing instead on a highly aesthetic, uncomplicated and idealized image. But design and construction needs to take myriad such details into consideration. Shell middens (mounds of deposits from shellfish harvested by indigenous peoples for centuries) around Darwin harbour

needed to be protected. There were also requests for observers from the local Larrakia and Wulna peoples during the construction of the Manton River crossing as it is a culturally and environmentally sensitive area.[56]

It would be a mistake to create an absolute polarization between a sublime Aboriginal sacred connection to the land and a superficial, crass, non-indigenous relationship, one mediated through modernity's transportation and communication technologies. Not only does this create stereotypes of both cultures, it effaces the multifarious and often creative contemporary engagement between a diversity of Aboriginal communities and the products of technological culture, from satellite broadcasting to bridges. For example, the small township of Fitzroy Crossing in the far north of Australia's Northern Territory has a mainly indigenous population.

The Fergusson River Bridge, Northern Territory, Australia, 1918, refurbished 2003.

A bridge over the tropical Fitzroy River was constructed as part of a 'Beef Road' to facilitate the transportation of cattle from the huge cattle stations of the region. A memorial marking the opening of the bridge has been decorated by locals to celebrate both bridge and involvement in the local industry.

As we have seen, it is a similar story in Tibet. Tibetan concerns about technological development as such were few and generally well-considered. The main issue voiced by Tibetans and their supporters in western countries lay with questions about power and decision-making. Who was the development for? What would the impact be on local communities? What kind of cultural imagination was being mobilized and imposed?

Close examination of both the Australian and Tibetan projects shows how crucial it is to give due consideration to the locale when it comes to bridge design and construction, whatever the size of the overall project. This is particularly important when it involves indigenous cultures, no matter how much the locale may seem to be in the 'middle of nowhere' or however seemingly 'remote'. Otherwise, within this scenario, the bridge, despite its beauty, can easily become a technology of power and domination. The ethics of complex systems relates to the inherent interconnectedness of all the parts. As has been seen, bridges sharply concentrate, focus and condense the railway or highway 'complex'. At the same time they transform such a complex, giving it new inflections and possibilities.

Fitzroy River Bridge Memorial, Northern Territory, Australia.

2 The Technology of Assemblage: Bridges and the Construction of the City

Introduction

Hiroshima's T-shaped Aioi Bridge was long famous throughout Japan due to its unusual shape. Spanning the Honkawa River and situated at the very heart of the city, the distinctive bridge made an excellent target for the Enola Gay in 1945, the US B-25 plane carrying the atomic bomb.[1] The world's first aggressive atomic blast occurred in the air about 300 metres from the bridge and, although severe damage was inflicted, it remained standing. In every direction, however, lay almost total devastation and countless bodies floated on the river under the bridge. Reconstructed immediately after the war, the bridge was eventually replaced in 1983. A few misshapen girders from the original structure, witnesses of the blast, were put on display in the Hiroshima Peace Memorial Museum.

The fate of the Aioi Bridge draws attention to the integral place of bridges in the story of the city. Like the bridge at Mostar, discussed in chapter Three, the bridge as target is fused with the city as target. Bridges are not just located *at* the heart of many cities but are often encrypted *as* the heart of these cities. It is this identification of the bridge with the city that has allowed it to be mobilized in promotional activities: tourism; local and global business; national and civic branding. In fact and fiction, the iconic modern city bridge is also the focus of concerns about contemporary terrorism. Rumours of plots circulate in the local media. From Brooklyn Bridge in New York to the Harbour Bridge in Sydney, surveillance and security has been tightened in the wake of the 2001 attack on New York's Twin Towers. In his 2005 thriller, *London Bridges*, James Patterson weaves a tale about devastating attacks, by an unlikely alliance of the Russian Mafia and Al Qaeda, on Queensboro Bridge (or Fifty-Ninth Street Bridge) in New York, Westminster Bridge in London and a small, unnamed bridge over the Seine.[2]

For over 200 years, the modern city has provided the milieu for the most densely complex codification, symbolization and spacialization of bridges. Although every type of circumstance has produced astonishing innovations in structural and architectural design, no other context approaches the richness and diversity of engagements with the bridge that the city has provided.

Poets, novelists, painters, photographers, musicians, film directors, social commentators and tourist promoters have repeatedly engaged with city bridges and thereby contributed to their phenomenology and meaning. While the city bridge has stimulated many examples of structural design and engineering achievement, the range of meanings it has constellated are overwhelmingly related to the changing visions of the city as a meta-context. While the bridge has been used as a lens or frame by which to view and understand the city, it also seems to condense, amplify and often transform these often complex meanings and issues.

Bridges are a technology both for mobility within the interior of cities and also for the modern city's expansion, its reach deep into rural landscapes and across national borders, as an inherently controlling, imperial and colonizing power. Cities are nearly always assemblages both of new areas and of pre-existing towns, villages, islands, locales. Bridges are crucial technologies that enable this gathering and linking to happen.

The circulation of people and materials dramatically increased in scope and scale with the advent of public transport, at first using horse-drawn omnibuses and then by means of steam-driven railways. The modern industrial city was intensely crowded and usually congested, with bridges becoming integral to the architecture of new public spaces. The addition of electrified light-rail and tram transportation late in the nineteenth century placed new demands and meanings on the city bridge.

By the 1920s and '30s most cities were faced with urgent questions about the impact of motorization. A quantum leap was thereby demanded in engineering technology, in the design and construction of city roads and bridges, as well as in their planning and architectural conception. This was a paradigm shift as immense as the one instigated by the invention of railways. In a matter of a few decades horse-drawn transportation retained only a faintest

London Bridge, shown in a stereograph of c. 1896.

trace of its former all-pervasive importance. The onset of the automobile coincided with the widespread utilization of new materials in bridge construction, in particular of reinforced concrete. While concrete itself is ancient, the late-eighteenth century invention of Portland cement, with its dramatic improvement in strength and durability, led to a renewed interest in concrete as a building material. The first unreinforced concrete bridge was constructed in 1816, in Souillac, France, and the first reinforced concrete bridge was built in 1889. By 1911, with the construction of the Risorgimento Bridge in Rome that spanned 100 metres (328 ft), the age of reinforced concrete bridges had truly arrived. By 1927 the French engineer Eugene Freyssinet had developed pre-stressed concrete, thereby opening the way for immensely stronger concrete bridges and considerably longer spans. New materials and the new, lighter, loading demands made by automobiles as compared with railways encouraged radically new designs and new construction procedures to emerge.

From the 1920s onwards there were basically three responses to the rise of the car and to what would quickly become a fetishism of automobility. Most ancient cities, such as London and Paris, tried simply to cope with the new demands while protecting their traditional cores. Existing bridges, designed primarily for railways, horse-drawn transportation and pedestrians, were modified where possible. New roads, designed specifically for automobiles, were constructed. These were mainly intended either to take traffic around the city (such as London's North and South Circular) or to move in a radial direction linking the urban centre outwards, often by means of roads, such as the parkways in the USA, that were radically novel in conception. These radial roads expanded the city into new satellite towns and suburbs. In addition, the urban centres were themselves being linked through new inter-city highways.

Paralleling these developments were sustained detailed critiques of rural disruption and the unplanned growth of strip development along the highway corridors.

While similar development through modifications of existing structures did occur in 'newer' cities such as New York and Sydney, these cities also tried to adapt to the automobile in more radical ways. New bridges, some of a spectacular scale, were constructed in the heart of the metropolis, along with inner-city expressways. London, so revolutionary when it came to accepting the immense reconstruction demanded by rail within the heart of the city, would wait until the 1960s before reluctantly accepting such roads and bridges within the city itself.

North Avenue Bridge spanning Merritt Parkway, Westport, Fairfield County, Connecticut, photographed after completion in 1940.

Finally, automobility seemed to offer some cities, such as Los Angeles, an opportunity and impetus for rapid growth such that the city itself became inextricably designed around the highways and their bridges. With improved commuter transportation systems, the expansion of suburbs and overwhelming car ownership, pedestrianism became a highly localized activity and underwent changes in meaning comparable to that instigated by the flaneur in the second half of the nineteenth century.[3]

Bridges and the invention of the cosmopolitan city (1800–70)

The modern city was a nineteenth-century invention. Its genesis occurred in Britain. In 1800 only 2.2 per cent of Europeans lived in cities with populations of more than 100,000.[4] Even in Britain more

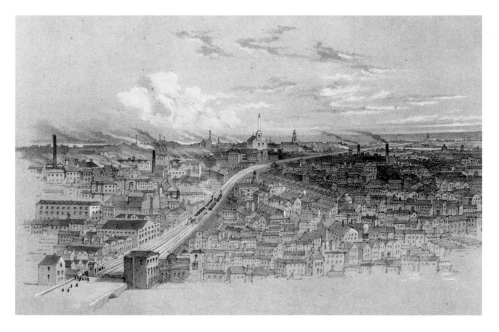

Greenwich Railway: bird's-eye view.

than 80 per cent of the population was rural in 1750, but by 1900 it was over 80 per cent urban. The dawn of the railway era in the 1830s provided the catalyst for the modern city. In the case of London, the world's first modern metropolis, railway corridors were carved through the existing fabric of the ancient city, greedily devouring land and destroying vast swaths of buildings. These radial transportation corridors moved vast numbers of people, with unprecedented speed and regularity, from outside the city into its very heart. In addition, rail corridors radiating from London connected urban centres throughout Britain and also, via port cities and steamships, across the Channel to continental Europe and across the Atlantic to North America. Other cities were also being connected by rail, with the first major inter-urban railway line being established in the 1830s between Manchester and Liverpool.

Highgate Archway Viaduct, London, 1840.

Similar developments took place elsewhere, with a rail link being opened in the 1850s from Chicago to the eastern seaboard.

Even before the impact of the rail, cities like London had experienced rapid growth under the dynamic regime of early industrialization. Mass public transport was suggested as one innovative answer to the daily challenge of repositioning the bloated population. By 1829 the horse-drawn omnibus was invented to cope with London's inner city transportation on a mass scale and the 1830s saw a huge increase in omnibus traffic. London's radial highways and bridges had to be upgraded in order to cope with this increase in horse-drawn traffic. John Nash's Archway Viaduct of 1813 drew on Thomas Telford's aqueduct designs and anticipated rail bridges of the 1840s. This traditional northern gateway to the city carried internal traffic over the main road out of London.

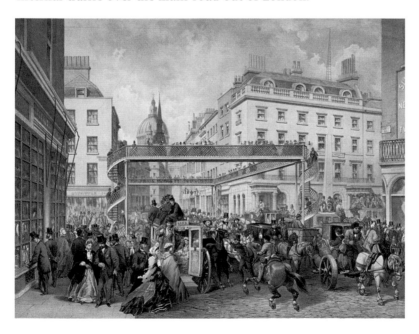

Design for a new footbridge at Ludgate Hill, London, 1862.

Between 1830 and 1850 London's population soared from 1,900,000 to 2,700,000. Railways brought increasing numbers of people and quantities of material into the city, which all had to then be moved around either on foot or by horse. The surge in the number of pedestrians required some way of organizing and separating different kinds of traffic. The flow had to be sustained and econom-

The first Southwark Bridge, London, completed 1819.

Waterloo Bridge, Evening, 1896, lithograph after a sketch by James Whistler.

ics demanded improved circulation both of people and goods. Ingenious designs were proposed, such as an imaginative pedestrian crossing at Ludgate Circus in mid-century London. However, social organization and civic leadership moved slower than technological innovation so that between 1830 and 1850 there was little change to major thoroughfares.

Between 1820 and 1830 a significant increase in steamboats on the Thames produced an urgent requirement for bridge crossings over the river that would cause minimum interruptions to river traffic. Ferries were totally inadequate to the task and a major programme of bridge construction began. London had acquired only three bridges over the Thames in 600 years. The oldest of these was the medieval London Bridge. Westminster Bridge was opened in 1744 and Blackfriars in 1769. Within three years, between 1816 and 1819, the number doubled: Vauxhall in 1816; Waterloo in 1817 and Southwark in 1819. Vauxhall Bridge, designed by James Walker, comprised nine iron arches each spanning 23.8 metres. Waterloo Bridge, designed by John Rennie, consisted of nine granite arches each spanning 36.6 metres). It was generally admired as a structure but charged tolls and was not a commercial success. In 1878 the Metropolitan Board of Works purchased it and scrapped the toll charge. Many of these bridges were demolished and replaced throughout the early twentieth century, either for structural reasons or to accommodate motorized transport such as the tram and automobile. In the case of the much loved, much painted 1817 Waterloo Bridge, upon its demolition and replacement in the 1940s, its stones were distributed throughout the Commonwealth as a symbolic gesture.

Machinery began to be used extensively for construction. This included steam engines that operated pumps for the cofferdams when the foundations were being built and for driving foundation

piles. Southwark Bridge, also designed by Rennie, incorporated what were at the time Britain's largest cast-iron arches. The centre span of 73.2 metres weighed a colossal 1,300 tons. As with Waterloo Bridge, machinery such as steam engines played an important role during construction. Over the next few years several other bridges were completed, including Hammersmith Bridge (1821–7), London Bridge (1831, rebuilt 1971) and Chelsea (1858).

An increasing population meant increased numbers of pedestrians and, along with horse-drawn traffic, this placed enormous demands on the inner city infrastructure. Traffic jams on London Bridge in its early years were legendary. Tolls on Southwark and Waterloo bridges discouraged their use. Hungerford suspension bridge, opened in 1845, was the only new one on this stretch of the river. It was built only for pedestrians. Despite a toll, three million people used it per year.

By 1838 three railway stations were operating in central London: London Bridge (for railways servicing Britain's southeast); Euston (servicing the midlands); and Paddington (with lines to the west). In 1848 Waterloo station was opened (connecting London with the country's southwest). By 1852 there were a ring of such stations

Construction of Blackfriars Bridge, London, c. 1864.

Hammersmith Bridge, London, c. 1896.

around Central London, on both sides of the Thames. Ways had to be found, not only efficiently to distribute incoming travellers throughout the city, but to facilitate cross-city travel between these railway termini.

These multiple crossings of the Thames, right in the centre of the city, had an immense impact on the shape of the metropolis. Sections of the city that had previously been relatively separate from each other were drawn together, creating something new. From Budapest to New York, bridges spanning the major rivers created very different cities. In Hungary the Széchnyi Chain Bridge was constructed between 1840 and 1849 and linked the two towns of Buda and Pest on opposite sides of the River Danube. In a sense this is how the city of Budapest was born. Both Buda and Pest had fallen to the invading Ottoman army in 1541 but suffered different fortunes under the Turkish occupation. Buda had been the previous capital of Hungary and had continued as the administrative centre of the region. Pest, on the other hand, was neglected and by the time of the reconquest in 1686 by the Austrian Habsburgs was substan-

Chelsea Bridge, London, c. 1860.

tially derelict. However, during the next two centuries it was Pest that boomed due to its vibrant commercial activity. The bridge, by joining these two very different towns, not only created the city of Budapest but also symbolized the idealized unity of the Hungarian nation. Similarly, by spanning the East River and joining Brooklyn with Manhattan Island, the Brooklyn Bridge, constructed between 1869 and 1883, virtually created the city of New York. The meanings and values attached to each side of these rivers resulted in a steep cultural gradient across individual bridges, from one end to the other. In Paris the Left and Right Banks had well-established and utterly different connotations. North or south of the river in London, too, carried divergent associations in terms of social class and significance. Each end of the Brooklyn Bridge connected to an entirely different sense of place and socio-economic order.

Széchenyi Chain Bridge, Budapest, opened 1849.

Industrialization resulted in the invention of new materials for bridge building. Stone arches were being replaced by wrought iron. This demanded new types of bridge design, new aesthetics and new technical apparatuses of construction. As already mentioned, steam power was becoming a regular feature of bridge construction. In addition, the entire 'profession' of engineering was undergoing rapid transformation with a new breed of engineers-as-heroes at its apex. Engineers such as Bazalgette were completely transforming not just the architectural shape of London but the very way it functioned as a whole. Indeed, this era marked the emergence of the professional engineer as a new, modern force and cultural icon. Under pressure to bring some semblance of order and control to an explosion of urban construction and development, new structures of urban governance also appeared, starting with London's Metropolitan Board of Works in 1865.

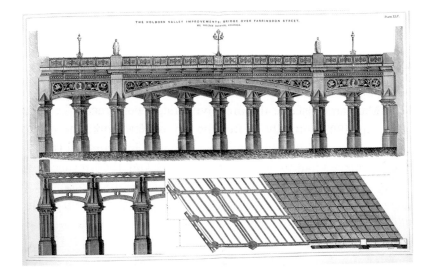

The Holborn Valley Improvements: Bridge over Farringdon Street in London, built 1863–9.

London's population surged again from 2,700,000 in 1851 to 3,900,000 in 1871. This unprecedented expansion contributed to a dramatic growth of the suburbs. The boom in London's inner city railways climaxed in 1863. Unlike the great London railway boom and mania of 1846 the population was getting less tolerant of the disruption caused by construction. Nevertheless, the need to cope with the traffic flow caused by this extraordinary influx of people and the need to transport and distribute them around the city placed extraordinary demands on inner-city bridges. New ones were built and older bridges were either widened or replaced. Holborn Viaduct (opened in 1867) was a precursor to a new type of large inner-city bridge. Older bridges across the Thames, such as the eighteenth-century Westminster Bridge – upon which Wordsworth composed his famous 'Ode' – and Blackfriars had to be replaced (in 1862 and 1869 respectively) by an upgraded design more suitable for the demands of increased traffic. The original Blackfriars Bridge, completed in 1769, was Italianate in style and consisted of nine arches made from Portland stone. The new 1869 bridge that replaced it is constructed from wrought iron and has five arches. Even this bridge

Ludgate Circus, London, 1881, with St Paul's beyond.

St Paul's Cathedral and Blackfriars Bridge, London, of 1869.

had to be widened between 1907 and 1910 from 21 metres to 32 metres to cope with increased traffic.

What were previously villages and small towns were stitched into the fabric of the expanding city and its suburbs. Bridges became conspicuous features.[5] The new transportation corridors, with their bridges, crudely intruded into pre-existing urban and pre-suburban townscapes.

Changing perceptions, changing representations

After mid-century, photography increasingly assumed the main documentary role for this urban and suburban transformation. Painting became increasingly free from this obligation and explored other dimensions of bridges, both aesthetic and experiential. Photography worked alongside industrial design and an industrial mode of production to transform the 'bridge' and how it was viewed. Stereoscopic views became fashionable, reinforcing as they did a sense of three-dimensional realism.

The new perspective focused on the way that the modern city was expressed through the bridge as a technology of mobility and

Bridge over Mare Street, Hackney, London, 1850s.

Steam train crossing a viaduct over a terraced street, Lancashire, 7 July 1968.

assemblage. Bridges were integral to, yet separate from, the road/rail system of the modern city. Bridges were also monuments and architectural forms in their own right. They created entirely new places – both within themselves and in their capacity to influence and gather the urban milieu around them. Novelists and poets, philosophers and artists used bridges as a lens for their reflections on this new complex and challenging phenomenon that was the modern metropolis. There was an outpouring of new ways of perception, reflections on new experience and attempts to find new meanings.

Representation – celebration and vitality

Many artists celebrated the dynamic vitality of the new city and its great themes, 'its kinetic activity, its juxtapositions and ironies, its massive forms and tiny details'.[6] Bridges also offered an elevated vantage point, a clearing both literal and metaphorical, amid the clutter, somewhere from which to view. They could provide spaces for reverie and reflection. Bridges were also stages on which a performance could be seen. Bridges could sometimes express a new urban intimacy, a possibility of new perspectives, of encounters in new types of public space and even erotic reveries.[7]

Bridges were frequently mobilized in literature and art as vantage points for reflection both on the city and on modern life in general. They seemed able to encapsulate the city's paradoxes and at the same time to offer a possibility of transcending the city. Wordsworth's famous poem 'Composed upon Westminster Bridge, Sept. 3, 1802' lay on the cusp of the city's transformation. Perhaps unbeknown to Wordsworth, his ode saluted the passing of the pre-industrial metropolis:

Earth has not anything to show more fair;

Dull would he be of soul who could pass by
A sight so touching in its majesty;
This City now doth, like a garment, wear
The beauty of the morning; silent, bare
Ships, towers, domes, theatres, and temples lie
Open to the fields, and to the sky . . . [8]

This contemplation on Westminster Bridge occurred at a crucial moment. It lay just before the spread of the industrial city around the world. Naples, Vienna, Berlin, Rome, St Petersburg, Budapest and Moscow were each to follow London and Paris in a massive growth spurt. The expanded pre-industrial metropolis exemplified by London provided the template for what was to follow.

Gustave Caillebotte, *On the Pont l'Europe*, 1876–7, oil on canvas.

St Petersburg was one such city, caught on the cusp of the modern. Dostoevsky, in his 1866 novel *Crime and Punishment*, used bridges as sites of hope, realization and reverie in the midst of despair and inner torment.[9]

Much of Paris in the second half of the nineteenth century had been transformed into the epitome of a bourgeois metropolis. Between 1852 and 1870 an intense programme of massive construction and demolition under the direction of Baron Haussmann had catapulted Paris into modernity. Some artists, such as the Impressionist Gustave Caillebotte, were drawn to the regimented networks of boulevards, built to facilitate the free flow of traffic, as well as to the railways with their grand central stations and industrial-design bridges. Caillebotte explored both the material forms of the new architecture and the particular daydreams they seemed to induce. He focused both on the experience of the new breed of flaneurs who strolled for pleasure through the delights offered by the modern city and on solitary individuals meditating from some vantage point. Both qualities are combined in his paintings of Le Pont de l'Europe, an immense iron bridge that spanned the railway yards of the St-Lazare train station. The painting of 1870–77 shows two men staring from the bridge, gazing through the monumental lattice girder that functioned as structural support. The main character, a middle-class man, looks away from the viewer and through the tightly organized, ruthlessly symmetrical iron grid towards the station beyond. He seems almost transfixed by the view. The uniform steely-blues and greys create a sombre almost melancholy mood, an atmosphere that is reinforced by the total absence of anything natural, as well as by the constrained and narrow perspective, the absence of horizon, and the tight, almost claustrophobic, cropping. The bridge is represented here not just a site *from* which to view but a frame *through* which to view. The bridge disciplines the gaze and the painting is an evocation of a newly emerging industrial-bourgeois perspective. Yet, Caillebotte's vision was neither pessimistic nor critical. He was curiously matter-of-fact. In another 1876 painting of this bridge-locale, a well-dressed bourgeois man and woman are casually promenading across the bridge on a sunny day. A more informally dressed man leans against the rail and gazes down through the lattice girder. The painting adopts an open perspective that leads into the city in the distance.[10]

Other French artists were drawn to the industrial qualities of the modern cities, particularly their bridges. Monet was fascinated by the effects of industrialism and the city, but in his case it was the smoky and foggy atmosphere, the effects of pollution caused by the extensive burning of coal. As Seiberling has noted, Monet shared his preoccupation with others, such as the author Hippolyte Taine. As early as 1860 Taine wrote of the ships and docks on the Thames:

> They are enveloped in a fog of smoke irradiated by light. The sun turns it to golden rain and the water, opaque, shot with yellow, green and purple, gleams and glitters as its surface lifts and falls, with strange and brilliant lights . . . The gleam of brown water river water, the diffusion of light trapped in vapour, the white and rosy luminosity playing over all these colossal objects, spreads a kind of grace over the monstrous city . . .[11]

London, as the world's first modern metropolis, with its characteristic dense fogs, especially around the Thames, attracted Monet, who spent several years there towards the end of the century, concentrating especially on the atmospheric play around Waterloo and Charing Cross Bridges.[12] Charing Cross Bridge had been con-

structed in 1863 for the South-Eastern Railway in order to carry trains and pedestrians across the river to Charing Cross Station. As Grace Seiberling points out, in its uncompromising industrial design Charing Cross Bridge took 'a quintessentially nineteenth-century form'.[13]

The underside of the city bridge

Monet was not only uncritical of the underworld of industrial city life, he was actually fascinated by the new aesthetic possibilities on offer, even in its polluted atmosphere. But authors such as Dickens and artists such as Doré were deeply disapproving of its social consequences. As the century progressed, a dark realism appeared in representations of the Victorian city. Increasingly, city bridges were often presented in a less than elegiac light.[14] Gustave Doré's *London – A Pilgrimage 1871* chronicled this London underworld, sharing a sociological perspective akin to that of Dickens or Engels. The underside of the bridge featured prominently in Doré's vision. At

Claude Monet, *Charing Cross Bridge*, 1903, oil on canvas.

times this was quite paradoxical, as in his portrayal of homeless men taking refuge beneath the arch of a bridge. While offering at least temporary shelter, the bridge also symbolizes the remorseless and heartless onset of modernity and of industrial capitalism. With the radical reconstruction of the city in full swing, with its new, increasingly controlled and commodified public spaces, Doré's image points to those meagre places outside or beneath the grid. A melodramatic and moralistic emphasis was often given to this realism, one that particularly utilized the underside of bridges and its popular associations. George Cruikshank's print series of 1848, *The Drunkard's Children*, includes a desperate suicidal jump, not surprisingly by a young woman, from a bridge.

Bridges were not just witnesses to the disruption being caused by construction and new patterns of everyday life in the city, but were instrumental to them. As Urry points out, 'the very building of railways flattened and subdued the existing countryside. The train was a projectile slicing through the landscape on level, straight tracks, with countless bridges, cuttings, embankments and tunnels.'[15] Crucially, this was happening not only in the rural regions but in the heavily built-up cities and towns. These railways with their bridges were also integral to the newly emerging urban and suburban landscapes. As Doré showed, the effects were not always salutary and in his nightmare-ish vision of urban working-class backyards the bridge carrying the railway overhead emphasizes the cramped and depressive immobility of the dwellings.

Raymond Williams cites Dickens describing London as a monster, as a new type of city, a centre of entrepreneurial capitalism, of greed and remorselessness, but nevertheless still a human construction and still with choices in terms of its future shape: 'Everywhere were bridges that led nowhere; thoroughfares that

were wholly impassable.'[16] There was scaffolding, bricks, construction, decay. 'In short, the yet unfinished and unopened railroad was in progress; and from the very core of all this dire disorder, trailed smoothly away, upon its mighty course of civilization and improvement.'[17] After an initial celebration of the dynamic growth of the city and its myriad possibilities, many became concerned about the loss of traditional ways of life. Under the sway of such sentiments the paintings of industrial bridges were often less popular than highly romanticized images of bridges far from the city environment.

Bridges and the invention of the Cosmopolitan City (1880–1920)

London's population surged again from 4,200,000 in 1875 to six million in 1895, while the number of traffic journeys increased at

Gustave Doré, 'Railways in London', from *London: A Pilgrimage* (1872).

an even faster rate. This period was the culmination of what Soja calls the 'third Urban Revolution', a massive expansion of the symbiotic relationship between urbanization and industrialization. New solutions to an overburdened public transport system needed to be explored.[18] New forms of mobility and new patterns of everyday life resulted in the development of excursion traffic

Joseph Pennell, *The Bridge at Hell Gate*, 1915, etching.

The Rhine Bridge, Mannheim, 1890s.

which also placed increased demands on the city's transportation infrastructure and led to continued construction of new bridges at its heart. These included the controversial faux-Gothic Tower Bridge over the Thames opened in 1894, the ornate Alexander III bridge over the Seine in Paris completed in 1900 and the monumental Hell Gate Bridge over New York's East River. This bridge opened in 1916, alongside the Manhattan Bridge which had previously opened in 1908.

Quasi-Gothic medieval features or those that echoed an ancient monumentalism tempered many bridge designs of this era, hovering as most societies were between a past that had been dominated by aristocratic nostalgias and more bourgeois-democratic-industrial futures. Unlike London's Tower Bridge and the Alexander III Bridge, the Hell Gate Bridge, which was an inspiration for Sydney's famous bridge some years later, more fully embraced a modern industrial aesthetics. Such an aesthetic vision, as with Gustave Eiffel's works

The Rhine Bridge with the Siebengebirge range in the distance, 1890s.

or Benjamin Baker's Forth Bridge, celebrated pure structure and made little attempt to hide either functionality or the massive materiality that pushed the industrial origins of the prime structural components into the foreground. In order to emphasize these features in the Hell Gate Bridge Gustav Lindenthal inserted visually impressive extra structural components, such as large spandrels above the lower chord of the arch that were redundant to the load carrying capacity. Another functional deceit designed to amplify the sense of massive scale was the construction of huge masonry towers at either end of the bridge which are in fact structurally redundant (a trope repeated at Sydney). Indeed, despite the overall commitment to a modern industrial aesthetics, Lindenthal was not entirely able to relinquish an earlier imagining as is witnessed by the arches, balustrades and cornices that adorn these towers.

Late nineteenth-century and early twentieth-century painters, drawing on any number of 'experimental' or 'avant garde' genres of painting, tended to avoid the darker visions of earlier years and instead used the bridges to explore a rich diversity of perspectives on the new and rapidly changing city and emerging urban experiences. André Derain painted colourful Fauvist depictions of Waterloo and Westminster Bridges in the first decade of the twentieth century. Monet's Impressionist interpretations of Waterloo and Charing Cross Bridges, deeply atmospheric in every sense but scarcely disturbing, have already been discussed. To these could be added more the introspective and psychological works such as Edvard Munch's existential *Girls on the Bridge* of 1901 or Lyonel Feininger's haunting urban painting, *The Green Bridge* (1909), in which the bridge, with its detached observer studying the street life below, introduced a kind of politics of verticality into a portrayal of the modern city, a new kind of gaze.

From the late nineteenth century onwards painting and photography were joined by cinema in the visual representation of city bridges. The earliest films that featured bridges were known as 'actualities'. As Chale Nafus points out, the development of lightweight movie cameras from 1895 onwards allowed scores of filmmakers to go out into the world and film anything they thought was worthy of note. Bridges were a popular subject for these extremely brief film clips. Unlike a still image of a bridge a movie allowed another order of spacial and experiential complexity. The movie allowed the viewer to be a participant. It could seemingly take the viewer across, under, or through the superstructure of a bridge. Understandably, given that New York was the principal base for filmmakers prior to Hollywood's development just before the 1920s, Brooklyn Bridge dominated these actualities. Initially with running times of scarcely a minute, these documentary snapshots treated viewers to *Across Brooklyn Bridge* (1899), *A Full View of Brooklyn Bridge* (1899), *New Brooklyn to New York via Brooklyn Bridge* (1899), *Panorama from the Tower of Brooklyn Bridge* (1903) and *Panorama Water Front and Brooklyn Bridge from East River* (1903).[19] Movies also allowed detailed coverage of the construction and opening of new bridges. With the arrival of feature films in the mid-1910s, bridges were often located in documentaries or travelogues, such as *The Bridges of New York* (1921). Bridges also began to be settings for drama, adventure and romance in feature films, such as Buster Keaton's civil war drama *The General* (1927).

With their huge audiences films not only familiarized large numbers of people with iconic bridges, they were initiated into a vision of the modern city through the frame of the bridge. Many bridges became synecdocs, a small part of something that symbolizes the entirely. In the immensely popular 1940 romantic-tragedy *Waterloo Bridge*, the bridge functions as a place of memory, of a fateful meeting and of romance. A wartime tale of a US soldier on leave and a struggling English dancer, it evokes and frames as so often is the case with bridges, the trajectory of a 'fallen' woman and hopeless love. The bridge itself is scarcely seen but a glimpse is sufficient to evoke complex and long-standing popular associations: it had been painted by numerous artists such as Constable and Monet, artists who were held in great affection and esteem. As one of the iconic bridges of London it signalled the intensity, energy and global centrality of the cosmopolitan city of London and its river – a premier financial, communication and commercial centre and a major port. It also summoned a deep nostalgia, one associated less with Empire than with 'little England' as manifested through its working, urban population. Popular 'travel' books of the 1920s and '30s celebrated the bridges over the Thames both as national icons and also as sites of soulfulness and nostalgia. In his series of essays from the 1920s, *London*, the prolific author H. V. Morton leaves what he calls the 'feverish' Piccadilly with its 'epileptic lights' and walks to the embankment and Waterloo Bridge. It is a cold, clear night and the river both sooths and lifts his spirit: 'The Thames at night is the most mysterious thing in London. So much a part of London, yet so remote from London, so cold, so indifferent, so wise.'[20] A policeman tells him that Waterloo Bridge seems to have a fascination for people contemplating suicide, especially women.

In the case of London, the sentiment accorded to the bridges over the Thames by its inhabitants and general population alike has been crucial to the city's identity. The replacement of much loved nineteenth-century classically-inspired structures such as Waterloo Bridge (in 1945) and London Bridge (in 1972) by modern steel and concrete designs, albeit graceful and efficient, both structurally and functionally changed the symbolic landscape of central London. Paradoxically, Tower Bridge, aesthetically much derided at its opening in 1894, has moved to the centre of London's iconography.

Automobility and the city bridge (1920-90)

Chicago's Michigan Avenue bascule bridge, opened in 1920, was one of the first planned responses to the influence the automobile was having on shaping the twentieth-century city. It was directly linked into the city's traffic system and gestured ahead to the extraordinary impact of automobility on all cities and their bridges. A new upsurge in the construction of major bridges was occurring within the heart of cities. In New York the George Washington Bridge opened in 1931. Sydney gained its famous Harbour Bridge in 1932.

Michigan Avenue Bridge, Chicago, photographed in 1987.

In 1900 there were 8,000 registered motor vehicles in the USA. By 1916 there were four million and by 1925 this had increased to over twenty million. Immediately after World War II the rise was even more pronounced and by 1955 there was a car ownership rate of one per family.[21] The extraordinary proliferation of the automobile effected a transformation of the modern city and its relationship to the surrounding rural regions as dramatic as the one instigated by the railroad. The influence on the bridge was no less profound. While eventually no city would escape having to respond to the dictates of the car, New York was in the forefront of this collision between city and automobile. 'From the 1920s and 1930s onward, the nineteenth-century infrastructural shell of New York City was gradually encased within an expanding network of new roads and bridges', writes Matthew Gandy, who points to the ways that this process 'hollowed out parts of the old city'.[22]

The early decades of the twentieth century were marked by the advent of 'technological modernism and regional planning' resulting in what Gandy terms 'scientific urbanism'.[23] Joseph Stella's 1917–18 Futurist paintings of Brooklyn Bridge pointed to the way in which these new sensibilities about scientific and technological progress were reinterpreting existing structures. Stella enthused that the bridge 'felt like a shrine to a new religion, a new civilization'.[24] Elsewhere the emerging vision of urban planning was bringing entirely new structures and systems into being.

From the 1930s onwards the 'impact of modernist aesthetics in the New York metropolitan region became associated with large-scale infrastructure projects such as roads and bridges', comments Gandy.[25] At the cutting edge of this modernist ethos was the development of landscaped roads, or what were termed 'urban parkways'. In the 1920s and '30s, the USA became a pioneer of the landscaped road or parkway, from 'tree-lined boulevards to the

regional extension of urban roads into sparsely developed frag-
ments of nature at the edge of cities, and finally, to the
development of a national network of federally promoted recreational routes'.[26]

The post-First World War emphasis on unimpeded travel along
landscaped roads was a development of ideas that had gained
currency through individuals such as Olmsted, who had been
working on his designs around the end of the nineteenth century.
Indeed, 'the first of a new generation of modern arterial parkways
specifically designed for use by automobiles was the fifteen-mile
Bronx River Parkway, completed in 1925'.[27] It had been conceived

Joseph Stella, *The Voice of the City of New York Interpreted: 'The Bridge, 1920–1922'*, oil and
tempera on canvas.

Merritt Parkway to New Haven, Connecticut, 1944.

originally by Olmsted in the 1890s. It was a unique kind of road, designed purely for leisurely purposes. It was almost a longitudinal park through which one drove to a similarly recreational destination. The goals of future urban freeways, of commuting, escaping or easing urban congestion, or satisfying urban transportation's urgent requirements, were not part of this unique concept. Heavily planted with trees the landscaped parkway corridor was envisaged as a 'scenic utopia'. Clean-lined concrete bridges were designed to fit into this vision. The parkway combined engineering as an art form with an aesthetics of landscape architecture.

Complex, multilevel interchanges have been around since 1858 when, as mentioned earlier, Olmsted built an overpass to separate traffic in Central Park. The first cloverleaf interchange was built near Woodbridge, New Jersey in 1928. The imperative behind the design and construction of modern freeways from the 1920s onwards, with the first limited access road in the USA being the 1924 Du Pont Highway in Delaware, was the demand for free flowing, uninterrupted traffic movement.

New York's circumferential parkway was completed in 1944, along with the impressive so-called 'pretzel' intersection. It included the Grand Central Parkway, the Grand Central Parkway Extension, and the Interborough Parkway. This was a multilevel road with five underpasses. 'The rural landscape became crisscrossed by turnpikes and interstate highways.'[28] In 1900, 39 per cent of the population in the USA lived in urban areas, but by 1920 this had jumped to 51 per cent. By 1960 more people lived in the suburbs than anywhere else. People could live considerable distances from work. Commuting became the norm for vast sections of the population and industries now followed the roads that ringed the cities. A proposal to construct an interstate highway

system was approved by Congress in 1956. 'The resulting loop and radial, limited-access, high-capacity roadway design was superimposed . . . on practically every American city.'[29]

Bridge design and construction had to keep pace with the expanding highway network. The Triborough Bridge of 1936, for example, was a project involving three bridges, and was a key component in the integration of Manhattan, the Bronx and Queens. Bridges also had to dovetail with and if possible enhance the aesthetics of clean lines and unimpeded flow that had been initiated by the parkways projects. There was an emphasis on speed and mobility. But these took a different form to the power-visions of pre-World War II Futurism. Gradually the aesthetics both of the landscaped parkways and of the experience of travelling along them, became normalized as part of the urban landscape. One commentator insisted that the 'space–time feeling of our period can seldom be felt so keenly as when driving . . . up and down hills, beneath overpasses, up ramps, and over giant bridges.'[30]

Triborough Bridge, New York, opened in 1936.

The underside of this vision was that drivers often became disoriented, or even lost, within these huge intersections, and considerable distances needed to be covered when negotiating a simple change of direction in the journey. The key thing to be avoided seemed to be stopping. Roads became known as 'paved ribbons'. The fantasy of speed and flow which came to dominate road design also captured the bridge, which became subservient to the road. A detailed text from the 1970s on engineering aesthetics says, 'A bridge must curve if the road curves, split if the road splits', and 'the continuity of [bridge] structure [must] emphasize the continuity of the road'.[31] It is recommended that bridges avoid any disturbance of a clean-lined silhouette. Even lamp posts have sometimes been condemned for destroying the aesthetic 'ribbon' effect. This quest for lightness is not reducible to functionality or economics; it is always a concern of imagination. The highway ribbon fantasy is one of anti-matter. Matter slows one down, while ribbons are light, almost bodiless – and they are clean. This fantasy was given its initial impetus through the aerodynamic aesthetics of the so-called 'Streamlined Decade' that followed the Second World War, when everything – cars, furniture, radios, as well as roads, buildings and bridges – came under an aerodynamic imagining.[32]

The USA was not alone in developing these streamlined highways and bridges. By 1935 the early road designs of post-Second World War Germany evolved into the first autobahn. With their advanced designs, they were conceived to be a mix of heroic engineering and works of art. In addition, drawing on a well-established mythology about the natural world, the incorporation of forests into the road and bridge designs was particularly significant for the Nazi regime. Everywhere during the interwar years there was a belief in technologically driven utopias. In Italy,

Overpass on an autobahn, late 1930s.

the autostrada emerged as early as 1922–30 as privately-funded ring roads around Milan. For the Fascist government the autostrada, like the autobahn for the Nazis, became a key symbol and evidence of the success of the prevailing authoritarian political and social ideology.[33]

These freeways, or ring roads and inter-city highways, with their limited access and hence requirement for multiple crossings, for complex intersections with numerous ramps to allow uninterrupted flow with no diminishing of speed from one highway to the next, devoured bridges at an unprecedented rate. A recent 'motorway', the M7 around Sydney for example, covering 40 kilometres, required the construction of 144 bridges. That is an average of one bridge every 300 metres, but each intersection consumes dozens at a time.

While a preoccupation with aerodynamics has now retreated into pure functionality, concerns with the fantasy of smooth flow continue to dominate the contemporary era. One of the few exceptions to the preoccupation with light, unobtrusive, free-flowing design were the bridges over the initial, 1960s section of the M1 from London to Birmingham, Britain's very first restricted-access freeway. The bridges – static, oppressive and monumentally heavy, unadorned reinforced concrete – were almost universally criticized as ugly. The designer, Sir Owen Williams, had been regarded as one of Britain's leading modernist designers before the Second World War. While Williams insisted he was guided merely by cost and function, for some it seemed as if he was being deliberately anti-aesthetic, setting up an opposition to the dominant modernist ideology of lightness and flow, a kind of counter-modernism.[34]

By the 1960s engineering science was confronted by limits to the finance being made available for large-scale bridge-building in the city. The design climate was increasingly complex and contradictory. Gandy suggests that in the USA at this time many 'symbols of modernity such as elaborate infrastructure networks, bridges, tunnels and public spaces had fallen into disrepair, their economic use and cultural meaning altered in an unfamiliar landscape dominated by new patterns of urban development'.[35] However, as Susan Robertson insists in her study of the construction and promotion of the Westway project in London, 'limited access highways' were still being 'considered as the epitome of modernity'.[36] The Westway project, opened in 1970, was a 2.5-mile raised highway that cut across established working-class housing, effectively a long bridge, a radial link between central London and the route to and from the west of England. Proudly celebrated by its supporters as a project that finally brought Britain up to the modern standards of continental European cities in terms of traffic infrastructure, it was also the site of protest about community disruption at a local level.

During this period, in visual art, the city bridge seemed to elude the critique being applied to modern cities. There were exceptions, of course. Echoing his 1906 painting, *Bridge in Paris*, with its single-minded focus on a dark tunnel-like underside, the American Edward Hopper's 1946 painting, *Approaching a city*, shows a similarly sparse, unpopulated entrance to an underpass. In marked contrast to Nash's triumphal early-nineteenth century gateway into London at Highgate, in Hopper's vision one enters a city through its underworld, its underbelly.[37] There is an unsettling eroticism in Hopper's moody vision of the city and its bridges. However, the paintings of bridges by the German artist Oskar Kokoschka offer a completely different vision of the city bridge. From Dresden in 1923, to Prague in 1934–5, to London in 1963, the energy and vibrancy of the city is highlighted through the bridge, with swirling masses of colour. His later bridge paintings move to an almost cosmic vision that is utterly centred around the form of major bridges.[38] The Australian artist Jeffrey Smart, on the other hand, while focusing on topics similar to Hopper, highlights the surreal, the spare rather than sparse possibilities in the geometric landscapes of the modern city. Paintings such as *Approach to a city, III* (1968–9), *The Cahill Expressway* (1962) or *The Underpass* (1986–7) are not introspectively anxious.

Jeffery Smart, *The Underpass*, 1986–7.

They do not depict alienation but sustain an intense curiosity in a solitudinous human presence within an architecturally formal urban landscape. While his paintings skew the taken-for-granted view of the world, they reveal an unexpected aesthetics.[39]

The bridge and the branding of the city

Over the past two decades dramatic fireworks displays around large, iconic, city bridges have become part of the synergy between corporate, national and civic interests. They are conspicuous exhibitions of power and aspiration. From Sydney to Hong Kong, London to Moscow, bridges are being integrated into the branding of cities and nations. In this process, if a city is fortunate enough to possess a major bridge, it is often promoted as their central icon. This is not an entirely new phenomenon. As has been seen, New York's Brooklyn Bridge has long been used to promote not just New York but the USA and a new global order. However, as Michael Silk puts it, 'globally induced economic upheavals have resulted in a process of intensified place-competition between cities, states and nations'.[40] This milieu of heightened competition has resulted in a constant process of branding and rebranding around markers that signal uniqueness and visual appeal: 'Place-specific differences, image and profile thus become weapons and provide competitive advantage in what have been called "place-wars".'[41] The struggle is not only for difference but also for definition as a 'global city', to be included in a network of such 'premier-league' cities within a global economy.

While key bridges have become mobilized in these place-wars, these structures go beyond being just images or signs for promotional representation. They are also crucial technologies of mobility for these place-wars. A bridge such as the immense Tsing Ma

Bridge in Hong Kong features in a range of promotional material, selling everything from tourism to investment opportunities. But, as will be discussed more fully in chapter Four, the Tsing Ma Bridge also radically affects Hong Kong socially and geographically. It connects Lan Tau Island to the mainland, is an integral aspect of the new international airport, and is a key link in the development of a Pearl River Delta mega-city. There is a tension between intensely local interests and the wider national and global impacts of a major bridge.

While spectacle and celebration have long been associated with major bridges, especially their opening, recent years have witnessed a steep rise in the varied occasions for increasingly grandiose, high-tech orchestrated displays. The intention of using such displays to present an idealized civic or national persona to the world is not new. However, contemporary image-saturated

The Tsing Ma Bridge, Hong Kong, under construction in the 1990s.

marketing has crossed new visual thresholds. The aim now seems to be to 'mobilize every aesthetic power of illusion and image in an attempt to mask the class, racial and ethnic polarizations going on underneath' in order to woo tourists and investors, or to promote a sense of, or belief in, local unity.[42]

Contemporary promotional culture, with its ready access to a rich media mix, presents an enhanced capacity to reframe the bridge. As Silk points out, 'spectacular structures and landscapes are abstracted from local culture and translated as symbols of the culture to be promoted beyond a nation's own borders'.[43]

With an upsurge in the popularity of bridge walking and bungee jumping, the bridge has also been effectively mobilized in a dual process of entertainment and promotion. Vertigo-inducing commercial tours for increasingly large numbers of intrepid tourists high across the top arch of Sydney Harbour Bridge, for example, allow a framing for both individual tourist and Sydney Harbour.[44]

The constant repetition of key bridges in advertising and in a variety of other promotional productions is integral to the branding of the city. They appear embedded in films and on postage stamps, in tourist brochures and on invitations to investment. Often they attempt to mobilize nostalgia in the service of a range of causes. The contemporary representation of these iconic bridges can be an attempt to negotiate a tension between a nostalgically re-imagined past and a radically different, often uncertain, future.

The bridge as installation

Development of the contemporary city bridge has moved in two important directions. On the one hand, the capacity to construct ever larger spans, carrying high-density, fast-flowing traffic, has allowed the creation of vast assemblages or mega-cities. While this has already been mentioned in terms of the Tsing Ma Bridge and the urbanization of Pearl River Delta, it is a development that will be discussed more fully in chapter Four. The other move taken by the contemporary city bridge has gone in the opposite direction. For some relatively small bridges, often for pedestrians only or ones which place pedestrianism high on the agenda, spanning capacity can be pushed into the background and the 'artistic', 'architectural' aspect can take precedence. With the technical and economic difficulties of spanning 'short' distances easily solved, these bridges offer the opportunity for a conspicuous display of form. The balance between engineering, architecture and art, which lies at the heart of bridge design, can undergo a crucial shift. These bridges are akin to art installations. This does not mean that function has taken a back seat; however, the precise nature of what constitutes the function of a bridge has shifted. In some ways it has circled back around and through a more medieval concept of the bridge, as places in their own right – as visual events, not merely as a technology of efficient crossing, nor dominated by rail or automobility. Small in scale, finely tuned to the requirements of intensely unique places and circumstances, they are highly visible in their individualized display of artistic, almost sculptural form. While large-spanning bridges can be often also objects of great individuality and beauty, these 'boutique' bridges represent one extreme in the spectrum of what David Billington terms 'structural art'.[45]

Santiago Calatrava is a major figure in the evolution of these types of bridge. He seems to move easily between architecture, art and engineering, assuming the role of artist, architect and engineer. New forms of material, construction and prefabrication are utilized in his unique designs. Calatrava refers to his bridges as

'structural compositions', overtly making links with artists and filmmakers in his approach to bridge design.[46] The creativity of his work was acknowledged with a 1993 exhibition at New York's Museum of Modern Art.

Calatrava's bridges are not set in stunning natural landscapes, unlike, for example, Maillart's. Instead, Calatrava stresses the places that, often neglected, lie on the edge of cities: 'Most often public works in such areas are purely functional, and yet even near railroad tracks, or spanning polluted rivers, bridges can have a remarkably positive effect. By creating an appropriate environment they can have a symbolic impact whose ramifications go far

Venice's first major new bridge in centuries, by Santiago Calatrava, nears completion in the summer of 2007.

beyond their immediate location.'[47] This sentiment is shared by many contemporary designers. The Pasarela peatonal en Petrer footbridge at Alicante in Spain, or Mossops Bridge at Enfield in Middlesex, England, were both specifically designed to revitalize marginal areas.[48] Calatrava suggests that 'building a bridge can be a more potent cultural gesture than creating a new museum'.[49] As he puts it, 'The bridge is more efficient because it is available to everyone. Even an illiterate person can enjoy a bridge. A single gesture transforms nature and gives it order.'[50] Despite creating bold designs, Calatrava suggests that bridges offer only limited scope for innovation given their very nature: 'You have the bridge surface, the arc that supports it, and the foundations, with each representing about one third of the cost.'[51] Symbolic issues are crucial. While numerous early modern bridges emphasized symbolism in their design and ornamentation, there has been a post-Second World War trend towards austerity and functionality. Calatrava insists that today 'we have to rediscover the potential of bridges'.[52] The deck of his Pasarela Urbitarte footbridge in Bilbao, Spain, consciously draws on the shape of a fish bone, while the Alamillo Bridge over a branch of the Guadalquiver River in Andalucia has a single backward-sloping pylon 142 metres high that is inclined at 58 degrees, identical to the Pyramid of Cheops. This sloping pylon has become a symbol of modern Seville.

The closing years of the twentieth century saw numerous such bridge projects, many directly linked to the dawn of the new millennium. One of the more famous was the Millennium Bridge in London, the first new bridge over the Thames in over a century and the first purely pedestrian bridge over the Thames for even longer. It became famous in part because of its location in the very centre of this global metropolis and in part due to the instability or 'wobble' experienced when first used by pedestrians in 2001.

While it was pronounced structurally safe, few people felt comfortable experiencing such large oscillations underfoot. In this case the emphasis on artistic form – the thinnest blade of light sweeping 320 metres across the river – had to be modified with extra stiffeners.[53] Several hundred miles further north, another Millennium Bridge was being completed. While numerous bridges have been constructed over the Tyne River at Gateshead in northern England, there had been no additions for over 100 years.

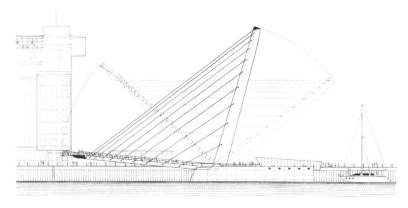

Gateshead Millennium Bridge.

Designed to accommodate both pedestrians and bicycles, the architects, WilkinsonEyre, drew upon both the symbolism of the human eye and its literal form. The unique design has a sweeping arch which can rotate or tilt along the axis of its entire length to facilitate the passage of ships. It was the winner in a 1997 competition run by Gateshead Council.

The construction of the northern Millennium Bridge was part of redevelopment of the area around the old docks. Known as Gateshead Quays, the area had been prosperous through the Industrial Revolution and Victorian era, and had been an important industrial focus for the region because of its very accessible port. Like many such districts, as the old industries went into decline in the 1970s and '80s so too did the once vibrant places associated with them. Associated now with riverside housing, shopping, entertainment, tourism and heritage precincts, the new bridge is a centrepiece in a strategy to regenerate – some might say gentrify – a pivotal but marginalized part of town.

Bridges like this one are part of broad civic strategies for developing both local areas and local pride. The scale is generally modest despite the innovative sculptural design. But a modesty of scale is definitely not a characteristic of the final example, a bridging development in Moscow. While older bridges in many cities around the world have been recast around shopping and entertainment precincts, the Khmel'nitsky Bridge is a unique case.

Between 2000 and 2001 two pre-revolutionary railway bridges, the Andreevski Bridge and the Krasnoluzhskii Bridge, were physically relocated from their original sites. In the case of the Krasnoluzhskii Bridge, the entire iron span weighing 1,400 tons was lifted off its original abutments and floated upstream to near Kiev Station. The equally massive Andreevski Bridge was floated downstream. There were no particularly strong reasons, neither functional nor symbolic, for where either was relocated. As Sabine Golz insists, rather 'than connecting points of attraction, they are the attraction. Created by a city government with an interest in a glamorous postmodern image for the city, they satisfy the demand for spectacle insofar as they themselves attract attention as historical-contemporary hybrids, as postmodern extravaganzas.'[54]

Originally built in 1903 and 1908 respectively, the Andreevski and the Krasnoluzhskii Bridges had been part of the Moscow city ring rail, taking the tracks over the Moscow River. They survived Stalin's reworking of Moscow's bridges, during which time most of them were replaced or rebuilt. Today the entire old span of the Krasnoluzhskii Bridge, now renamed Khmel'nitsky Bridge, is encased in glass. It has been transformed into an elegant, sophisticated glassed-in pedestrian shopping mall, an arcade, complete with polished wooden floors that one enters upwards by escalator. In her attempt to unravel the juxtaposition of shopping arcade and bridge in a new millennium global city Gölz understandably evokes Walter Benjamin's classic study of the late-nineteenth century Parisian arcades. Certainly, like the arcades in Paris over a century ago, the Khmel'nitsky Bridge clearly demonstrates the

Bohdan Khmel'nitsky Bridge, Moscow, now a mall.

consumerist-driven economies and cultures of the cosmopolitan city. It also signals the need for distinctive, spectacular icons, in order for the city to compete in global place-wars. Above all, it shows the resurgence of walking in the city and the 'architectural' struggle over the street as memory and culture.[55]

As a hybrid mix of old and new the bridge links past and future of the city. Gölz calls it a site 'for urban self-reflection'.[56] These bridges are integral to the attempts to redefine Moscow as an international metropolis, a global city and as a showcase of the new Russia. Given the ambitious scale of the scheme, there is an understandable tension between the civic and national governments.

Walking the bridge

At a purely local level, the construction of these sculptural pedestrian bridges in numerous cities around the world reflects a new emphasis on city walking. Even bridges designed also to accommodate automobiles often include enlarged spaces with seating where pedestrians can pause, congregate and rest. Perhaps this is a sign of a new flaneurism, a reworking of the late nineteenth-century phenomenon where people, predominately men, would stroll the modern cities attracted by the new public spaces and city life, with its heterogeneous crowds, civic architecture, cafes and shops. The new bridges of the late nineteenth century were one important site within the spacial reordering of the modern city that provided both a location for promenading and a frame for observing this phenomenon. By establishing new connections, new relationships between previously separated parts of the city, these contemporary 'boutique' bridges facilitate changes in the time/space/rhythm of selected zones of cities.[57] They initiate a remapping and thereby affect the relationship between body, place and memory, creating intimate zones of

public space, often highly regulated and commodified, but never-theless often still the sites of contested imaginings, creative engagements and chance encounters.

Brooklyn Bridge, New York.

3 Technologies of Connection

The bridge as border-technology

Early in 2004, a simple blue and white steel bridge, replete with customs post, over the Bug River near the town of Terespol in the east of Poland, became the extreme eastern point of the boundary of the new European Union. Commonly referred to as the EU, this is *the* contemporary economical-cultural-political paradigm by which modern 'Europe' is defined. Over the Bug River is Belarus, a part of non-EU 'Europe'.[1] Ancestral fears about Europe's vaguely defined, vulnerable, eastern border were, and still are, quietly condensed into bridges such as this one. It marks an ancient demarcation and defensive boundary zone. Centuries of anxiety about invasion from 'the East' contrast with promise of eastward economic and political conquest, plus the lure of territorial expansion by some European nations. From one end of the bridge to the other lies a steep gradient of wealth and power, human rights and democratic freedoms. Eco-political alliances of trade and defence, as well as definitions of sovereignty, begin and end at the bridge.

With the acceptance of several former eastern-bloc countries into the EU, the bridge instantly became part of 'fortress Europe', marking a boundary between the mobility-rich and the mobility-poor. Like castle gateways these bridges are necessary but vulnerable. They are heavily monitored and guarded moments in the defensive walls. At a time of perhaps unprecedented global movement of people, when 'illegal' migrants, refugees and asylum seekers are often lumped together and viewed by many with deep suspicion, anxiety and often hostility, the Bug River bridge, and many others like it, is also a practical-symbolic conduit across the divide. It symbolizes hope for many people at both ends of the bridge. From one side there is hope of a better life, while from the other is the hope of a more compassionate and less selfish and paranoid society. The bridge embodies the possibility of 'conversation'. It acknowledges that intercourse is possible and even desirable, or at least acceptable, between the two separated zones. What passes over this bridge, or else is refused passage, is a defining characteristic of the global order at the turn of the millennium.

Bridges are technologies of connection, of movement across boundaries and frontiers, of gathering. They are also markers of separation and division, technologies of surveillance and exclusion. They are technologies both of mobility and immobility.

While they have often been the focus of hope, from the most practical level to the most spiritual, generating powerful associations in the imagination of healing and reconciliation, at times bridges have been the specific target of vehement protest. The Skye Bridge in Scotland, for example, completed at the end of the twentieth century, seemed to threaten the famous island's islandness and cultural uniqueness. Around the same time, the construction of the Hindmarsh Island Bridge in South Australia was seen by many as a continuation of colonial arrogance and entrepreneurial greed, which threatened the religious beliefs and practices of already marginalized local Aboriginal women. This chapter will focus on these two case studies.

The bridge as gift

Like the bridge over the Bug River in Eastern Poland, the Columbia Friendship Bridge marks a highly controlled and constantly challenged boundary between immense wealth and poverty, that between the USA and Mexico. Diverting heavy traffic from Laredo in Texas and Nuevo Leon in Mexico, it is little known and used by tourists.[2] As a 'friendship bridge' perhaps it is an attempt to create a resonance around the positive associations of the bridge: to join; to overcome differences; even to heal. As if in an attempt directly to mobilize the bridge as a metaphor of connectedness and harmony, there have been numerous such 'friendship bridges'. Sometimes these have been a joint enterprise, a kind of mutual gift, between two neighbouring countries. Elsewhere, they have been a present from a wealthy donor, either another country or, in some cases, a corporation. The briefest of surveys reveals that the bridge as gift can be both a constructive exchange and a disruptive provocation.[3]

As gifts, bridges are potent expressions of practical aid to underdeveloped nations from wealthier countries.[4] Begun in November 1991 and completed in February 1994, the Mekong River Bridge was such a gesture from Australia to Laos and Thailand. Part of Australia's aid programme, the US$30 million two-lane 1,174-metre (3,851-ft) concrete bridge, with provision to carry future rail traffic, had both practical and symbolic intent. At the inauguration of construction in 1991, the Australian Minister for Trade and Overseas Development hoped that the bridge would 'light a path of peace in the region and inspire others to take changes, to go the extra distance that was required, if we were to create a new era of peace in Indochina'.[5] In keeping with its development aims, alongside twenty Australians in the labour force were 400 Laotians and Thais. While the response was overwhelmingly positive, a 1994 seminar was convened to look at any negative impacts of the bridge, including the flow of HIV/AIDS, traffic build up and accidents. It has been claimed that the 'bridge has become one of the most powerful and true symbols of peace and stability that has emerged in Indochina for decades'.[6] It quickly entered tourist guides. By the third anniversary of its completion, in 1997, celebrations were unequivocal: 'In one stroke the two halves of Southeast Asia, separated since the dawn of time by the river, were joined. Old divisions were put to rest and a vision of cooperation was anchored as solidly as the concrete pylons obtruding from the silty water. The mighty Mekong had been bridged.'[7] With thousands routinely crossing each year, the tenth anniversary was celebrated with fireworks. This bridge has its roots deep in Australia's problematic involvement in South East Asia, especially as a combatant in the Vietnam War. It dovetails with Australian desires to be considered more a part of Asia, almost as quasi-Asian. The appearance of the bridge on an Australian postage stamp reinforces its importance for Australia's national identity.

In many cases the bridge is a mutual gift between neighbours of equivalent wealth. As a hope for peaceful co-existence as much as a promise of increased trade and communication, there are many examples.[8] The Luzon Hydro Friendship Bridge in Ilocos, in the Philippines, was part of a corporate rather than a government initiative with a local community.[9] The company claims the bridge shows its commitment to local host communities and to the principle of corporate responsibility. When trans-national bridges are given as gifts, it can be difficult to unravel the truth from PR spin.

At times the 'friendship' aspect seems a distant hope or a diplomatic euphemism. In February 2001 it was reported that many people had been killed after heavy fighting and shelling between Thai and Myanmar/Burmese troops near Tachilek, and that the

Burmese authorities had shut down the Thai–Burmese Friendship Bridge again.[10] The Termez Bridge, or so-called 'Friendship Bridge', over the Amu River connecting Afghanistan and Uzbekistan had been built by the Soviet Army in 1982 to supply the military in Afghanistan. The bridge had been closed several times between 1996 and 1998 as the Taliban had come to power. In 2001 and 2003 it was reopened. The bridge was crucial for humanitarian aid to reach the difficult northern regions of Afghanistan. It also, perhaps, helped to overcome animosity and distrust on both sides. But in 2004, after bombings in Tashkent and Bukhara, it was closed by Uzbekistan due to concern about a flow of Islamic fundamentalism from Afghanistan.[11] The Sino-Korea Friendship Bridge across the Yalu River carries pedestrian, rail and road traffic. As one of the only ways to enter North Korea, it is a cautious and heavily controlled crossing.[12]

For Tibetan refugees the Friendship Bridge between Nepal and Tibet can be positively dangerous. Oppressive and violent actions by border guards from both China and Nepal against Tibetan refugees trying to cross the Tibet–Nepal border have been well-documented over many years. Few would be reassured by placards at the Chinese border post insisting that 'The People's Armed Police of the high plateau are honest and loyal guards stationed at the border to protect the nation and render meritorious service'.[13] Time and again, the bridge reveals itself as a border technology that both resists and filters 'unwanted' global mobilities, as well as enhancing the mobility of the select and privileged.

Ponticide at Stari Most

The crucial position of bridges in war is well documented and has been central to numerous movies. The construction, defence and destruction of bridges by opposing forces dates back to ancient times. Bridges are also targeted less for overtly military purposes than for psychological warfare against civilian populations. The most infamous such assault on a bridge in the past few decades was the deliberate destruction of the ancient bridge at Mostar, Bosnia-Herzegovina in November 1993. This was probably one of the most media-covered acts of architectural-heritage terrorism. Rich and intensely complex associations circulated around this bridge, before and after its destruction, as well as during its subsequent reconstruction. As a seminal global example of what Suha Ozkan has termed 'urbicide', it was on a par with the destruction by the Taliban of the ancient Buddhist statues in North Afghanistan.[14] The deliberate targeting of architecture as a form of control, as an integral part of religious or 'ethnic cleansing', and as a conspicuous demonstration of power, has a long history.

Completed in 1566 by the Turkish architect Hayruddin for the Ottoman emperor Suleyman the Magnificent after his conquest of the Balkans, this single-arch stone bridge was integral to the city of Mostar's role as an intercontinental crossroad between East and West. The bridge stimulated trade and communication. Mostar means 'Bridge-keeper' and the city, with its several bridges, became a meeting place for Muslims, Catholics and Orthodox Christmas, for Serbs and Croats. This masterpiece of Ottoman architectural engineering came to embody the success of social and religious tolerance, although, as Ivo Andrić suggests in his novel *The Bridge over the Drina*, perhaps this 'tolerance' was enforced unequally by a harsh but distant power.[15] It is difficult, especially in the aftermath of tragedy and loss, to unravel truth from nostalgic idealization. Nevertheless, Suha Ozkan insists, the bridge had 'merged two neighbourhoods into a single town and brought two groups into a single community'.[16] The bridge also assumed an iconic status in the history of bridges whether as an accomplishment of engineering, architecture, or art.

In the 1993 Bosnian war, hundreds of architectural monuments were deliberately targeted and destroyed. Unlike the devastating bombing of bridges by NATO during the Bosnian campaign, the targeting of architectural monuments had limited, if any, tactical or strategic military purpose. Its function was cultural humiliation, erasure and ethnic cleansing. The Convention for the Protection of Cultural Property in the Event of Armed Conflict, signed at The Hague in 1954, following the devastation of World War Two, was simply ignored, making this architectural destruction a form of war crime.[17]

Certainly bridges, as 'powerful symbols of connection in this region' were central in the conflict and it has been suggested that the systematic targeting of architecture in Bosnia-Herzegovina was 'an architectural cleansing', an act of 'cultural genocide'.[18] The destruction of the Stari Most and the outcry over it was a condensation of the widespread architectural destruction not just in Mostar but in the whole of Bosnia-Herzegovina. During the conflict there were confrontations over numerous bridges between militants from various ethnic groups. But at Mostar, where all of the town's bridges were destroyed and the old Muslim town remorselessly bombarded by the HVO (Croatian Defence Council) and where nearly every building was damaged, the ferocity seemed to be unparalleled, as if there was a hatred of any possible friendship, any future reconciliation. Apparently it took several attempts to obliterate the bridge. In his article, 'The Destruction of Stari Most', Suha Ozkan writes that on the morning of 9 November 1993 the bridge was deliberately shelled and destroyed by Bosnian Croats. Residents had desperately tried to protect the bridge: 'Automobile tyres were hung from the parapet to try to absorb the shock of the shells and reduce damage.'[19] Suha Ozkan denounced the destruction as a 'hatred of memory'.[20]

The subsequent reconstruction of the bridge at the end of the war was a deliberate attempt at healing and reunification both by local and international communities.[21] As early as December 1997 personnel from a Hungarian technical military unit serving in Bosnia had identified and removed original stone blocks from the river, but the reclaimed stones were found to be too shell-damaged for re-use. Nevertheless, as the next best thing over 1,000 new blocks were fashioned from the Tenelija quarry, the sixteenth-century source of the original stones.

The Old Narenta Bridge, Mostar, Bosnia-Herzegovina, photographed in the 1890s.

While reconciliation meetings were attempted between religious leaders and between concerned people in the divided communities, others tried to delay reconstruction, wanting to maintain a now ethnically divided city with its two communities permanently separated on either bank of an unbridged gorge that was itself a potent symbol of distrust and suspicion. As Nicholas Adams, in his article, 'Architecture as the Target', writes, the destruction at Mostar was both 'a symbol of loss in wartime and a symbol of hope for peace'.[22]

Over and above its practical function, or the esteem given to it as a great work of medieval engineering, or its place almost as a sculpture within the opus of world art, or even its symbolic role in bringing together communities that elsewhere were mutually hostile, the Mostar Bridge was experienced as something sacred by many. Here was a trace of ancient associations – the bridge as spiritual technology, as sacred architecture.

Forgiveness and reconciliation have at their core a spiritual, religious or sacred dimension. The bridge as a technology of connection and gathering can mobilize and enable this possibility. In the urge to seek its destruction and in the desperate attempts to save it, in the surge of support to reconstruct it and in the mourning of its death, Stari Most has reached deep into the imagination. Christine Evans, covering a 2001 arts festival in Belgrade, reported on a performance by the assertively multi-ethnic Mostar Youth Theatre, entitled 'The theatre of war, the murder of bridges'. It was said that the 400-year-old clay from the collapsing bridge 'stained the river red as it fell . . . We don't say it was destroyed, we say it was murdered.'[23]

Protesting the bridge: Hindmarsh Island

With a length of around 2,500 kilometres the Murray is Australia's longest river and with its tributary, the Darling, flows for about 3,700 kilometres, forming one of the longest rivers in the world. With its source in the Snowy Mountains on the east of the continent the river winds its way westward for most of its length before turning sharply south, heading toward the sea for its final 200 kilometres (120 miles). Just before reaching it, the river opens out into a huge system of lakes, lagoons and islands. While the Murray has deep and complex associations in the 200-year-old history of Australian exploration and settlement, the relationship between the river and the many indigenous peoples who have lived along its banks for over 50,000 years is of an entirely different order of profundity. The country of the Ngarrindjeri people encompasses these lakes, lagoons and islands where the river meets the vast Southern Ocean. The largest of the islands, separated from the mainland by the main channel of the Murray, is Kumarangk, renamed Hindmarsh Island by the earliest white settlers. The indigenous peoples of the Murray suffered greatly during the colonizing process, but, despite these depriva-tions, a small community of Ngarrindjeri maintained an unbroken connection with this land.

For most of the history of white settlement, the flat and often windswept Hindmarsh Island was considered small, remote, incon-sequential and out of the way by most South Australians and was virtually unknown outside the State. It was long the site of a hand-ful of farms, plus a few holiday homes and fishing shacks. However, in common with most developed countries, during the last decades of the twentieth century Australia experienced a real-estate boom in the demand for coastal properties, especially those within comparatively easy reach of urban centres. Marinas started to spring up in unlikely places to cater for the increasing numbers of relatively affluent yacht owners. New seaside developments were built for retirees and for those who just wanted to escape the city, as were second or holiday homes, as well as investment properties. In this climate, developers turned to Hindmarsh Island and sought state government permission, not only to build a marina and a coastal village there but, crucially, to replace the small, slow car-ferry with a bridge. The result was one of the longest and most divisive battles over a bridge construction in Australian history. It was a struggle that pushed the limits of the fragile reconciliation process between indigenous and non-indigenous Australians, and which exposed deep, fundamental, even irreconcilable, differences between two world views, two ways of law and two notions of what a bridge can actually mean.

In November 1988 a bridge emerged as a condition demanded by the developers if they were to go ahead and construct a marina on the island. The conservative-led South Australian government, desperate to stimulate this kind of development, promised to pay for the construction of the bridge.

Despite an apparently satisfactory environmental impact report and due consultation with Ngarrindjeri leaders to receive their approval, by late 1993 serious opposition began to be voiced against the bridge. While some supporters of the development tried to dismiss the opposition as an alliance of environmentalists, ferry workers and affluent owners of holiday homes, the truth was more serious. Ngarrindjeri women elders claimed that they had not been included in the original consultations, a common omission in such negotiations in the past where male anthropologists talked exclusively to indigenous males and where the sacred and ritual culture of indigenous women had been marginalized or just omitted in much anthropological study. The women elders claimed the bridge would interfere with what they called 'secret women's business' on the island, thus beginning a highly contentious battle, fought out in Australia's highest law courts and across all the nation's media, in university departments and scholarly publications, as well as in public protests, that lasted for over a decade. It quickly formed into a contestation between the ethos of commercial development and indigenous spiritual beliefs.

Protests began late in 1993 as attempts were made to stop construction commencing. In addition to lawsuits and demonstrations, early in 1994 the United Nations was asked to intervene. While concerns were expressed that the construction of the bridge would have a detrimental effect on a culturally significant landscape, much wider issues were condensed into the bridge and it now provided a sharp focus for general unhappiness about both the government's and mainstream society's attitudes to Aboriginal heritage.

At the core of the dispute lay secret information in a sealed envelope. A white female anthropologist was entrusted by the Ngarrindjeri female elders with demonstrating why the bridge posed such a threat to the indigenous women's culture. But indigenous law insisted that such knowledge was secret and could not be revealed to men, and preferably not even to non-initiated women. It could not therefore be made public knowledge. The sealed envelope was tendered in court as evidence. The developers had already invested considerable funds in the project. Along with their supporters, which included the state government, they were incredulous that a multi-million dollar development should be threatened on the basis of claims that could never be revealed, neither to them nor to the general public. However, Australia at this time was beginning to emerge from a long silence about the terrible treatment of the original inhabitants during colonization and settlement. As one report after another detailed a host of injustices, an intense renegotiation of Australian identity was initiated. In particular a deep uncertainty, anxiety and guilt arose within mainstream society about the founding plan and the legitimacy of white settlement. It also triggered a widespread desire for and process of reconciliation between indigenous and non-indigenous people. This (un)settling of Australian culture resulted in an uneasy, often ambivalent and contradictory relationship to itself and to the land, one in which intense confidence and independence vied with uncertainty and anxiety.

In mid-1994, within this deeply sensitive climate, the federal government ruled in favour of the Ngarrindjeri women. Out of respect for the cultural beliefs of the women the government minister responsible did not open the sealed envelope and therefore did not read the report, nevertheless he still banned construction of the bridge for twenty-five years. Indirectly it was reported that the secret business had something to do with fertility. It was intimated that the shape of the river channel between the island and the mainland resembled a uterus and that the women, drawing on traditional spiritual beliefs and knowledge, feared that a bridge would block this passage. Certainly as a place where salt and fresh water met it was site of special significance and fertility. From the Ngarrindjeri women's point of view the construction of the bridge would physically damage the channel and cause a disturbance to the life-giving waters of the Murray mouth.[24] At this point the developers insisted that the secret women's business which no-one could read was just a recent spur-of-the-moment invention and sued the state government who in turn attacked the federal government over the ban. A small group of dissenting Ngarrindjeri women elders then came forward to claim that the secret women's business was indeed fabricated, that it had been made up by men to prevent the bridge from going ahead. Claims and counterclaims were bitterly contested, as the Ngarrindjeri community was ripped apart and as accusations of foul play and unscrupulous practices were made towards media commentators and scholars on both sides. Suggestions that construction would create 1,200 new jobs and generate over $100 million had to be balanced against claims of interference with indigenous women's sacred sites and a threat to the credibility of Australia's process of acknowledging and protecting them.

Throughout the 1990s a bitter debate raged over Aboriginal spiritual beliefs and their place in a modern Australia undergoing a difficult process of reconciliation. The 'bridge saga' was tearing at the fabric of modernity and its foundations in law, social science and development. In addition, the struggle over the Hindmarsh Island bridge began to unearth reservations about the imagination of modern engineering and its technological products.

After numerous twists and turns, the ban was dismissed and construction went ahead. The resulting concrete bridge of ten spans, each typically 33 metres long, opened in March 2001.[25] Several thousand people from all backgrounds marched over the newly opened structure in support of about 100 Aboriginals who held a silent protest.

By whose logic was the bridge built? Questions arose not only about whose interests were being served by an ethos of development, but about what is meant by the term 'development'. Were sacredness and development necessarily opposed? It seemed difficult for many non-indigenous people and for the law to comprehend that the women's objection was both environmental and spiritual. A deep gulf was shown to exist between two divergent ways of knowing and of imagining human participation in the natural world. The bridge focused and concentrated a range of issues whose implications and relevance are not only confined to Australia. Beyond issues of power and the nature of development, the whole post-Enlightenment and modernist imagination came under question: What kind of technology is a modern bridge? Has its sacred and mythological power been lost in the 'developed' world? What are the consequences of a radical de-sacralization of bridges? Was it really so hard for most non-indigenous people to re-imagine the bridge, to credit it with profound ritual efficacy? How is the site of a bridge and our relationship to it to be imagined? What does it mean to own land?

The sadness that a few long-time island residents felt over a loss of island-ness following the construction of the bridge went virtually unnoticed. This was not the case in the next example.

An unwanted connection? Over the bridge to Skye

Around the same time as the Hindmarsh Island bridge saga was unfolding, another struggle over a proposed bridge was taking place on the other side of the world. This too involved connecting an island to the mainland and was also being fought by a minority group that had deep associations with the land, whose culture and language had long been marginalized and who were uncertain

Hindmarsh Island, South Australia.

whether the proposed bridge offered threat or hope. As with the Hindmarsh Island context, deep, albeit profoundly different, mytho-poetic associations were involved.

When is an island not an island? According to rumours in 2003 about new criteria produced by the European Commission, it is when the previous 'island' becomes connected to the previous 'mainland' by a bridge. Such was the controversy which threatened the island status of Anglesey in Wales and Skye, Bute, Muck and Rum in Scotland.[26] Locals pointed out that as England, Wales and Scotland form an island and that a tunnel connects it to France, does this mean that it is no longer an island? Does a tunnel have the same status-changing capacity as a bridge?

In late 1987 there had been urgent calls from across the community on Skye, the largest island off the coast of northwest Scotland – one of Europe's poorest regions and an important centre for the survival of the Scottish Gaelic language – for a decision to be made about replacing the ageing ferries with a bridge, and obtaining funding from Europe for its construction. Despite failing to acquire funding, the campaign for a bridge intensified.

The proposal to construct a bridge to connect the island with the mainland touched a sensitive nerve, not only locally but also nationally and internationally. Skye has a well-defined romantic identity around the world. It depends heavily on tourism, with visitors drawn in by the rugged mountain and coastal landscapes, by its clan history, by its reputation as a 'misty island' and by its associations with the romantic legend of 'Bonny Prince Charlie'. It is also the centre of the small, besieged and vulnerable Scottish Gaelic language and culture. But, while a bridge would extend the tourist season by overcoming the serious weather-dependency of the ferries and at the same time eliminate the long queues that regularly formed in the high season, it also went right to the heart of longstanding local issues and grievances. Concerns were voiced about the erosion of traditional Gaelic culture with an increased influx of incomers, about a loss of local independence, overcommercialization, a rise in crime, and damage to the environment.

One otter colony illustrates the way diverse environmental discourses were condensed by the bridge. The west coast of Scotland is home to about 700 otters, designated an endangered species, about 5 per cent of which live close to the planned bridge. One of the foundations was to be located on a small islet, Eilean Bhan, or 'otter island'. But the concerns went beyond conservation. A 1960 best-seller, *Ring of Bright Water*, had detailed the author's friendship with an otter. A very popular film of the book had been shot on location and many older people were familiar with the beauty of the landscape.[27] An alternative approach route to the bridge was suggested, as was building otter-proof fencing along the approach road and digging otter tunnels under the road. There were also other environmental concerns – local fishermen were worried about an increase in the current under the bridge and shellfish growers were anxious about the bridge disturbing their livelihood.[28]

A letter to the editor of the local newspaper succinctly put the practical arguments for a bridge: it would lower the costs of goods from the mainland; increase market choices for crofters and fishermen; greatly assist emergency hospital cases; and remove queues at the ferry during the height of the tourism season.[29] Between 1987 and 1995 the imagined bridge exposed deep fissures and tensions, as well as alliances between various groups on the island. Some saw the bridge as a waste of money that would have been better spent helping the many impoverished locals rather than the more prosperous inhabitants with their cars and regular journeys to and from the mainland.

The bridge proposal also raised the entire topic of transportation in the Highlands and Islands region, especially about an increase in car use and a decrease in the quality of public transport. Some queried whether the generally narrow Skye roads could even cope with the expected increase in traffic. Others tried to script the struggle over the bridge into a sharp polarization between radical and conservative visions of the island, between pro-independence pragmatists on the one side and nostalgic, romantic, traditionalists on the other. The reality was more complex. Radicals and conservatives, locals and visitors, romantics and pragmatists, could be found lining up on either side of the bridge proposal.

A 1994 survey conducted by the local hotels association indicated that 40 per cent of tourists would have their perceptions of Skye changed by the bridge and that the bridge would discourage 25 per cent of tourists from visiting more often.[30] While tourists recognized the advantages of a bridge, such as getting more out of the scenery and no ferry queues, they also stressed a loss of individuality, romance and landscape, more traffic on the island's roads, and increased crime. Despite a dismissive attitude by some residents, the question of tourist perceptions was a sensitive and critical issue.

Some locals voiced another deep concern, arguing that the bridge would increase commercialization at both ends and have a catastrophic impact on the culture, language, religion and traditional 'Gaelic' way of life. Once again, a proposal for a bridge raised the issue of development versus tradition as a sharp, highly polarized dichotomy.

The debates about the bridge, and especially about possible toll charges, became focused around the heated question of Scottish independence. A free bridge became increasingly synonymous with a 'Free' Scotland.

As early as 1990, numerous rural, conservation and art organizations expressed serious reservations about the visual impact of the bridge on the famed beauty of the view. There seemed to be two directions designers could go. On the one hand, a spectacular bridge could be built that was itself a conspicuous landmark. On the other hand, a structure could be designed that was visually of low impact, not very interesting, even dull. In bridge terms these two options equated to either a relatively cheap, thick, flat box girder or flamboyant cable-stayed structure with high towers and slender deck. It was generally agreed that engineering function and architectural form must coincide otherwise flamboyance would seem artificial and merely decorative, an empty and intrusively ornate gesture. However, the span was larger than the box girder construction was originally designed for, which would result in a thickness that would not be aesthetically satisfying. As a compromise, improvements to the box-girder design were suggested. But even this was criticized. The box girder design was labelled ugly, even a monstrosity.

However, construction of a privately funded toll bridge began in July 1992. The following year some frustrated locals turned to direct action. Thirty anti-bridge demonstrators, from groups such

Skye Bridge, Scotland.

as Skye Earth Action, were arrested while protesting about the disturbance to the otters and other environmental intrusions, as well as against the proposed toll charges. With completion imminent in 1995 there were reports of a 'bomb plot' by 'tartan terrorists', as well as various local boycotts being planned for the opening ceremony.[31]

The completion of the bridge was a national event. From London the *Guardian* newspaper reported the placing of the span's final section: 'Engineers will spend the next few days dumping cement on to it [the bridge section] and the imagination of everyone who has ever hummed the Skye Boat Song'.[32] The bridge had taken three years to build at a cost of £35 million, was 570 metres long, and could carry both road traffic and pedestrians. The bridge was officially opened on 16 October 1995. Alongside celebrations there were numerous protestors who refused to pay the toll.

The bridge continued to attract national attention long after the opening. In 1997 a survey found '50 cars a day turning away from the toll barrier, the vast majority saying the crossing was simply too expensive'.[33] Other visitors insisted that the bridge had made little or no difference to the island-ness of Skye, and that it remained a world apart despite being linked to the mainland by bridge. Protests continued well into the new millennium, mainly focused around groups such as SKAT (Skye and Kyle Against the Tolls, founded in October 1995) until the toll was removed in September 2004.[34] My recent visits to the island suggest that the ease of transportation provided by the toll-free bridge has been warmly welcomed by many residents. Other benefits and problems are less clear. But the Skye Bridge clearly shows that a bridge connection, whether free or at a cost, is not always greeted as an unequivocal blessing.

Bridges and the politics of verticality

The Israeli architect Eyal Weizman describes a recent plan whereby a projected Palestinian State is imagined as a number of separate territories connected by tunnels and bridges. He criticizes this scheme as an example of a more general principle in Israel whereby 'First' and 'Third' Worlds are 'spread out in a fragmented patchwork: a territorial ecosystem of externally alienated, internally homogenized enclaves located next to, within, above, or below each other'.[35] Within such a scheme, the border ceases to be one unbroken line and is instead a succession of separate boundaries and checkpoints. Israeli roads and infrastructure connect dispersed, discrete, well-guarded settlements, either by soaring over the pockets of Palestinian land by means of bridges and elevated highways or passing underneath them by means of tunnels.

In particular, Weizman focuses on Israeli settlements in the West Bank, which he describes as dormitory suburbs that rely on so called bypass roads connecting them with urban centres in Israel. These roads literally bypass Arab towns. With three million Palestinians thereby left locked in isolated enclaves, attempts were made to separate the Israeli and Palestinian traffic networks, preferably without them crossing each other. Territory was imagined three-dimensionally, with ethnically, politically and strategically defined regions layered one on top of the other. The West Bank was physically partitioned (three Jewish, three Arab), 'into two separate but overlapping national geographies in volume across territorial cross sections, rather than on a plane surface'.[36] Weizman calls this action that divides a single land area into a series of territories, a 'Politics of Verticality'. He insists that this three-dimensional system of roads and tunnels, of overpasses and underpasses, is critical for the partitioning.

At one point, where the separate transportation networks cannot avoid crossing, a 'Tunnel Road' connects Jerusalem with the settlements of Gush Etzion and further on, with Jewish neighbourhoods of Hebron. To achieve a separation of the systems, the road has to be carried by a bridge over a Palestinian cultivated valley and then go under the Palestinian Bethlehem suburb of Bet Jallah by means of a tunnel.[37] Together, these form the longest bridge and longest tunnel in Israel. Under such circumstances the border stretches along a horizontal plane or line. While limited Palestinian sovereignty extends to the valley and the city, the road, with its bridge and tunnel, is within Israeli jurisdiction. Weizman concludes that in the West Bank, 'bridges are no longer merely devices engineered to overcome a natural boundary or connect two impossible points. Rather, they become the boundary itself, separating the two national groups in the vertical dimension.'[38]

Weizman's analysis of the way bridges are being conceived and used as border-technologies in Israel points to a more widespread, albeit perhaps less concentrated and systematically planned, phenomenon. In this scenario bridges are technologies that create boundaries as multilayered vertical cross-sections, rather than technologies that connect or separate two sides of a border, each side imagined to be sharing the same horizontal plane. Increasingly First World cities have Third World centres – dangerous places of poverty and violence, as well as of cosmopolitan vitality. Cities and suburbs continue to be fragmented into discrete pockets of varying degrees of wealth, opportunity, health and safety. There is a danger that highway overpasses and underpasses, bypasses and through-routes are not only designed to improve the flow of traffic. They can also be integral to a politics of verticality, one in which engineering is used to create multiple, layered, but mutually disconnected, albeit geographically co-existing, worlds of territories and flows characterized by vast inequalities.[39] Indeed, as Grady Clay points out, the very construction of such highways, especially if elevated or in the form of overpasses, creates what he calls 'sumps', places both *outside*, as well as metaphorically and often physically *beneath* the more privileged flows and affluent zones. They are frequently well-policed, and often defined along ethnic grounds.[40] These are the internal borders under construction across North America and Europe.

Once again, building a bridge raises crucial questions about development and who benefits, about divergent and contested fantasies of 'development', 'land' and 'mobility'.

Walking the bridge: framing protest and reconciliation

As discussed in the Introduction, the bridge, both as material fact as well as metaphor and symbol, has an ancient and profound

Tunnel-Bridge, Israel.

connection to notions and practices of protest and of healing. Walking in a group, one that disrupts the normal traffic flow across a bridge either in a demonstration or celebration has a long history. The walking is enframed, concentrated, focused and intensified. Bridges can provide a stage. But more than this, the walking activates a key aspect of bridge-ness and of bridging. Reconciliation embraces all aspects of this tension, requiring as it does an engagement with both protest and healing, a joining of opposing positions, a transcendence of issues and values that divide and separate. Walking across a bridge can be a performance of hope.

Along with hope, reconciliation must, by necessity, engage with disturbing emotions, memories, responsibilities and a messy lack of closure. These are complex and untidy equations that are sometimes difficult to bring into focus and to be expressed. By using a bridge for a mass public display, both as a stage and as a symbolic form in its own right, the issues and sentiments can be given a clear and bounded frame while at the same time being amplified.

On Sunday 28 May 2000, a well-publicized and organized 'people's walk for reconciliation' took place over Sydney Harbour Bridge. Various estimates suggested that somewhere between 150,000 and 400,000 people from all sections of Australian society, including senior politicians from every major political party, Aboriginal leaders and church groups, walked the 4.1-kilometre route across the famous bridge. It was an event repeated across bridges in all of Australia's major cities. The date marked the official conclusion of a decade-long process of reconciliation between indigenous and non-indigenous Australians. Ranked as one of the great healing moments in Australian public life, all reports suggested there was a genuine feeling of hope and expectation. Many

were calling for a formal apology from the Prime Minister (who was conspicuously absent from the bridge walk) and a formal treaty between indigenous and non-indigenous peoples.[41] Sydney Harbour Bridge was well chosen as it has a long established iconic place not just as the centrepiece of Sydney, but of Australian cosmopolitan identity both for Australians and internationally. It was a photo opportunity for national and international media. The bridge functioned as a media frame as well as a space for reflection and a stage on which people could actively make a public statement of commitment.

Later that year, just before the Sydney Olympics, Nelson Mandela came to Australia to speak at World Reconciliation Day. He specifically cited the Sydney Harbour Bridge walk as evidence of a country 'wanting to heal itself and deal with the hurts of the past' and encouraged Australia to actively tread this path.[42] Perhaps significantly, the Mandela Bridge in Johannesburg, another symbol

Strikers crossing London Bridge, c. 1910.

of moving on after a long process of reconciliation, was opened in 2003 on the day of Nelson Mandela's eighty-fifth birthday.

Conclusion

The Peljesac Peninsula curves out like a hook from the coast of Bosnia and Croatia. It runs mostly northwards parallel to the shore from which it is separated by a relatively narrow stretch of water. The peninsula is part of Croatia, but close to where it joins the coastline there is a small enclave of Bosnian territory. This is because, while Bosnia is basically separated from the coast by Croatia, a small finger of Bosnian territory reaches out to the sea and gives Bosnia its only access to the Adriatic, where lies the port of Neum. However, this finger of Bosnian land effectively divides Croatia into two parts. Croatians travelling between the more southerly region and the northern have to cross this thin corridor of Bosnian territory. With tensions still simmering between these recent foes, fresh from an appalling conflict that was so much about territory and identity, this was never going to be a satisfactory arrangement. The peninsula, which is joined to the southern half of Croatia, bypasses the Bosnian enclave and stretches northward, running parallel to, but separated from, the northern half of the country. The obvious solution was to build what would be Europe's second longest bridge, between the peninsula and the other side of the narrow gulf thereby allowing easy movement between northern and southern parts of Croatia without requiring travel through Bosnia. The problem is that the wrong design would limit the size of shipping able to access the port of Neum and hamper the development both of the port and of Bosnia-Herzegovina. Protracted negotiations ensued from 2005 onwards to develop a design that would satisfy economic desires as well as the demands

Reconciliation walk over Sydney Harbour Bridge, 'Corroboree 2000'.

of reconciliation.[43] Within these border scenarios, the bridge is often entangled by competing and often contradictory demands. Reconciliation and healing, economic development, local and national territorial-based identities and mobilities are all condensed into the bridge – into its design, construction and in some cases its very existence.

4 Spanning Technologies

Given that the spanning capacity of a bridge, like the vertical height of a tower, is its defining characteristic, it would seem obvious that the span of the bridge should attract the most attention of any feature, be celebrated and admired above all other aspects. However, it is really only modernity that has seen this unprecedented focus on span size. Of course, the new structural materials of the industrial age, the associated social infrastructure and developments in computation allowed for – even encouraged – ever longer spans to be built, but these are insufficient reasons for the modern, almost obsessive, adulation of span size. For the last two centuries it seems as if there has been a competition. During this period, a simple quest for the longest span has fragmented quickly into a plethora of league tables ranking the longest particular type of bridge designated according to structural type: steel box girder; steel span truss; concrete box girder; concrete arch; steel cantilever truss; steel arch; cable-stayed; suspension; moveable and so on.

In musical terms these huge, often extraordinary, bridges, from pioneering examples of the mid-nineteenth century to the superbridges of today, are the symphonies and operas. Audacious in their conception, they inspire awe and enthusiasm. Vast amounts have been written about them. Their technical specifications are readily available, particularly through a plethora of internet sites and glossy books. Their images proliferate across numerous genres from postcards to postage stamps, from commercial and tourist promotions to movies and novels. Most have their own fan base that has been boosted in the past few decades by extensive online resources, bridge-blogs and quasi-fanzines.

Individual encounters with these massive bridges can be awesome, particularly at first meeting. While bungee jumping or an organized walk – linked by safety harness to other members of a group high across the topmost superstructure – can provide an extreme thrill, more everyday practices can also generate profound experiences. Many have experienced the tremulous possibilities, ranging from exaltation to dizziness, inherent in crossing a structure such as the Sydney Harbour, the Golden Gate or the Brooklyn on foot. Even a crossing by car, bus or train, particularly as one moves to the very centre of the span and any material support seems to fall away to an absolute minimum, can be nervously exhilarating. Cinema has regularly drawn on this range of experiences. In Alfred Hitchcock's *Vertigo*, for example, the immense span of the Golden Gate Bridge looms at critical moments as a signifier of vertiginous fear and challenge.

The Transcendent Span

Throughout the nineteenth century and into the first half of the twentieth, this obsession with span was partly a celebration of an engineering that was imagined almost heroically, a visible display of the mastery of materiality and nature, and of the success of industrial-imperial expansion. The increasingly longer spans were also integral to modern capitalism's revolutionary economic, social and political development. Running parallel to this practical intent ran

philosophical, aesthetic and religious sensibilities that either celebrated the control of materiality through the bridge or dissolved the
same materiality into light and spirit.

Overlapping this quest for the longest span, but not entirely
identical with it, has been the challenge of spanning the previously
unthinkable, and generally spectacular, obstacles. The nineteenth-
century mission to seek out ever-increasing challenges to span
intensified through the twentieth century: the Menai Strait; Avon
Gorge; the Mississippi River; The Zambezi River at Victoria Falls;
the Firth of Forth; New York's East River; Sydney Harbour; San
Francisco's West Bay; the Straits of Mackinac in Michigan; and
numerous other daunting valleys, rivers, lakes and estuaries. In the
late twentieth century, the spanning of awesome natural divides has
been supplemented and perhaps even replaced by the challenge of

Clifton Suspension Bridge and Avon Gorge, opened 1864.

joining what had previously been thought of as irrevocably separated: Sicily and mainland Italy; Asia and Europe; Hong Kong and
Macao; Russia and the USA; Sweden and Denmark.

It has been suggested that 'a new political and physical animal,
the multi-billion-dollar mega infrastructure project', has emerged
in recent decades.[1] The European list of such mega projects is
impressive in itself. It includes the Oresund Bridge between
Denmark and Sweden; the Vasco da Gama Bridge in Portugal; the
creation of an interconnected high-speed rail network for all
Europe and cross-national motorway systems, each with multiple
bridges; the fixed link across the Baltic Sea between Denmark and
Germany; and links across the Strait of Messina. Elsewhere there is
a similar story: the Akashi Kaikyo Bridge in Japan; numerous
bridge-related mega projects in China from Hong Kong to Tibet;
Malaysia's North–South Expressway; Thailand's Second Stage
Expressway; several such projects in the USA; Canada's
Confederation Bridge; the Sao Paulo–Buenos Aires Superhighway;
the Bi-Oceanic highway across South America from Pacific to
Atlantic Oceans; the Venezuela–Brazil Highway; even a $50 billion
project to link the USA and Russia across the Bering Strait.
Thoughts about this last project go back over 100 years, with the
designer of San Francisco's Golden Gate Bridge, Joseph Strauss,
putting forward perhaps the first serious proposition. Still only a
speculative dream, it could consist of three separate bridges using

Proposed bridge over the Strait of Messina, Italy, a 'view' from Calabria.

the Diomode Islands as a stepping stone to join Cape Dezhnev in Russia with Cape Prince of Wales in Alaska.

The super-spans that are often integral to these projects are understandably the focus of acclaim but also of high risk and threat. Cataclysmic structural failure, massive financial overspending and global terrorism haunt these new super-bridges. While in the nineteenth century the long-span sometimes symbolized the arrogant confidence both of capitalist and nationalist ideology, it was at times also an expression of a grand philosophy. Hegelianism and transcendentalism is given form in Roebling and the Brooklyn Bridge, or Thomas Pope's 'Rainbow Bridge' of 1811, while a vision of equality and common humanity is expressed through Thomas Paine's bridge designs. Even in the twentieth century the meanings of long-span bridges has sometimes been linked with an idealistic philosophy. David Billington's thesis, that there is an inherent relationship between bridge design and socio-political formation, has already been discussed in the Introduction.[2] But the philosophical underpinnings of the mega-span and super-bridge are of a different order. They relate more to global mobilities and flows, to national branding in an era of global place wars.

Zygmunt Bauman argues that this new mobility is fundamental to what he terms the 'Great War of Independence from Space', and that it is an indicator of a crucial new form of social stratification and power. He insists that these mega projects represent core developments of infrastructure. Mega bridges are integral to building an *infrastructure* of global mobility, to what Bauman calls a 'Zero-Friction Society', one that possesses an unprecedented ability easily to move people, goods, energy, information and money, at speed, over vast distances, in complex networks. This infrastructure, he argues, is bringing about a 'new politics of distance'.[3] With extraordinary new materials, new technologies of design and construction,

new models of funding and techniques of project management, the mega-spans are driven by a techno-logic of development that is sometimes at variance with practical demand. The Humber Bridge in England, for example, one of the world's longest spans, opened in 1981 but has been under-used ever since. Understandably, many have questioned the rationale for its construction.

Whether suspension or cable-stayed, pre-stressed concrete or box-girder, these super-spans seem most appreciated as something to look at, particularly by photographers, as a dematerialized visual aesthetic sensation, rather than a visceral one of direct physical engagement. There is a certain kind of awe at the audacity of the connection. But the centre of these giant spans is rarely a point of reverie.

Rion–Antirrion Bridge, Greece, opened 2004.

One Hundred Years of Span

A sample chronology of the first 100 years of this quest for span reveals brilliant experimentation in design and in the development of new materials to solve the many problems facing ever-longer spans. It also showcases individual engineers as heroic artists, auteurs or maestros. However, as early as 1873, the author of a book on long-span bridges critically warned that 'the size of a bridge is too commonly the popular standard by which the eminence of its engineer is measured'.[4]

- Thomas Telford's Menai Strait Bridge of 1826 was a wrought-iron chain suspension construction with a 177-metre (580-ft) span. At the time it was the longest spanning structure in the world. However, unlike most of the subsequent long-spans during the next 100 years, it was not required to carry the demanding burden of rail traffic.

- In the 1850s I. K. Brunel's Maidenhead Bridge with two main arches each of 39 metres was the world's longest brick arch span. It also carried the longest major rail line in the world – the Great Western.

- Robert Stephenson's unique tubular Britannia Bridge of 1850 comprised two spans of 140 metres. It was competely over-designed (and expensive) as a direct response to the disastrous collapse of the bridge over the Dee. There were major doubts in 1840s about the reliability of suspension bridges to carry rail traffic. They were considered to vibrate and sway too much, especially under excessive loads and in strong winds.

The bridge was designed to carry the Chester and Holyhead railway over a tricky and strategic stretch of water. The rail connected with ferries to Ireland, a place of commercial and, with ongoing unrest, of military importance. It was considered one of the most significant construction projects in the world in the 1840s. The Royal Navy insisted that there could be no interference with shipping through the strait, no obstruction at the centre of the channel and no loss of clearance at the banks. Arches were therefore eliminated as a possible option. At the same time, as a commercial venture, the trains needed to run on time, sticking to timetables and with a high degree of reliability. The solution: a huge wrought-iron tube over 9 metres deep and almost 4.5 metres wide, through which the trains ran. It was not a comfortable solution for the passengers. Drawn by coal-powered engines, the density of smoke, trapped by the tunnel-like tubes, was appalling.

- Brunel's Royal Albert Bridge at Saltash, completed in 1859, had similar constraints placed upon its design to those placed on the bridge over the Menai Strait. Brunel's solution consisted of two enormous wrought-iron tube arches, each spanning over 140 metres. The tubes were oval in cross-section, 5.1 metres wide and 3.73 metres deep, from which the deck was supported using iron hangers. The main spans of the Britannia Bridge contain about 50 per cent more iron per unit of length than those of the Saltash Bridge. The cost of Brunel's bridge was half that of Stephenson's. Many have been of the opinion that Brunel's bridge is aesthetically superior because it clearly shows how the structure functions whereas Stephenson's masterpiece hides it.[5]

- Gustave Eiffel was innovative in his use of wrought-iron and steel, creating the cost-efficient aesthetics of the Garrabit Viaduct in France, which spanned the deep gorge through which flows the Truyere River. Given its location in the Massif Central, his design had to contend with extreme winds, something at which Eiffel was expert, having already designed other large bridges using his unique focus on aerodynamics. Opened in 1884, with a 165-metre span, Eiffel took advantage of a steep drop in the price of steel to build with this strong material. At 122 metres, it held the record for many years as the world's highest bridge.

- John Roebling's Niagara suspension bridge of 1855, with a span of 250 metres was extraordinarily cost-efficient and extremely light. Roebling was a champion of the suspension bridge and was determined to show it was an appropriate design to carry rail traffic. He was also convinced that wire cables were the way of the future rather than the chain-links used by the British. The cable spinning techniques he perfected at Niagara (and made into a family business) went on to form the basis of his much longer Brooklyn Bridge. With its unique double deck, accommodating rail with road underneath, the structure was extraordinarily stable for a suspension bridge. As a final stabilizing feature the deck was not only attached to the two main cables by means of vertical wire stays

but also by extra wires attached along the length of the bridge deck converging onto the top of the towers. As completion approached, Roebling heard of the Wheeling suspension bridge failure and stiffened his Niagara Bridge even more. He used extra cables running diagonally down into the gorge to prevent any chance of the kind of buckling of the deck seen at Charles Ellet Jr's Wheeling Bridge. Roebling then went on to lead the reconstruction of Ellet's bridge, as well as to design and construct the Cincinnati Bridge over the Ohio River, which was completed in 1866. This consisted of a 322-

Wheeling Bridge over the Ohio River, West Virginia, opened in 1849.

metre span, with iron wire cable suspension, and was the world's longest spanning bridge at the time.

- The Brooklyn Bridge, which has already been discussed at length, opened in 1883. This was John Roebling's masterpiece. With a main span of 486 metres it was easily the longest suspension bridge until 1903. In many ways the Brooklyn Bridge is a kind of Ur-case for long-span bridges, not only because of its structural characteristics and its global centrality, but primarily due to the vast wealth of narrative material that has accompanied it. The construction of few other major bridges has been documented so fully in the public imagination. Perhaps no other bridge includes such a family dimension in its construction – both triumphant and tragic. Importantly, the story of the construction of Brooklyn Bridge constantly draws attention away from the 'span-ness' of the immense span and even from the soaring heights of the towers. With John Roebling already killed while working on the bridge, his son Washington carried on in his place but was severely crippled by extended exposure to extreme pressure in the caissons while supervising the digging of the bridge-tower foundations. He was confined to his room, watching the construction through a telescope, while his wife Emily increasingly took over the supervision and project management. The crippling of Roebling forces us to take notice of the foundations. As any engineer will confirm, attention to the foundations is not merely a structural requirement but a critical perspective on the bridge. Foundational issues overwhelmingly determine both location and structure of the span. In the case of Brooklyn Bridge, such activities, usually hidden away, the least spectacular and visible part of a long-span bridge, are both moved to the foreground and populated. It is here that the drama of family and workers begins to unfold.

• Opened in 1874, James Eads's St Louis Bridge had a length of 480 metres. Its three steel arches, each spanning over 150 metres were of an unprecedented size for constructions other than those adopting suspension designs. It was the first use of steel in a structure of this scale. The broad river, with its vigorous tidal currents, muddy bed and even thick ice in winter, posed huge problems. In addition, the free passage of paddle steamers up and down the river had to be guaranteed. Eads used pneumatic caissons in the construction of the mid-river foundations. Twelve workers died from compression sickness or the 'bends'. This was Eads's only bridge and the expense of the structure, coupled with its under-utilization, caused the company formed to build it to go quickly bankrupt. Nevertheless the bridge achieved instant symbolic status as the first to cross the iconic Mississippi and its aesthetics were almost universally praised. The poet Walt Whitman wrote, 'I have haunted the river every night lately, where I could get a look at the bridge by moonlight. It is indeed a structure of perfection and beauty unsurpassable, and I never tire of it.'[6]

• The Forth Railway Bridge of 1890 was designed by Benjamin Baker. Like Eads this was his only bridge. A cantilever truss construction, its main spans of 521

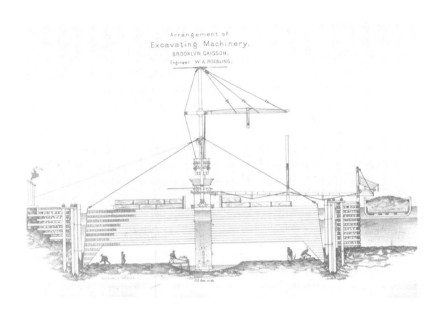

Arrangement of
Excavating Machinery.
BROOKLYN CAISSON.
Engineer W.A ROEBLING.

metres were longer than Brooklyn's. Also, the height of
the bridge was unprecedented, not just clearance under
the span but the towers. Brooklyn's were 84 metres
while the Forth Bridge structure topped 104 metres.
Impressed with its superior strength, Baker utilized steel,
which had only just been approved as a legal construction material in Britain. While the bridge is now
acknowledged as a masterpiece, there was considerable
controversy at the time about whether it was massively
over-designed or just monumentally massive. Baker had
one eye firmly on the collapse of the Tay Bridge in 1879
and he was determined to avoid such a calamity.

The quest for ever longer spans continued into the twentieth century
with one innovative design after another. The Hell Gate Bridge over

Excavating Brooklyn Caisson.

the East River in New York was, at 298 metres, the longest spanning arch when completed in 1916. Lindenthal, a Moravian migrant to the USA, had previously overseen completion of the Williamsburg Bridge (1909), redesigned the Manhattan Bridge (1909) and designed the Queensboro Bridge (1909). It was one of the last long-span bridges to be built in the USA purely for the railway, thereby signalling the advent of the automobile age.

The George Washington Bridge in New York, designed by Swiss-born Othmar Ammann purely for automobiles, was completed in 1931 and at 1,067 metres was twice the span of any previous sus-

The Forth Bridge on a 1928 railway poster.

pension bridge. Originally Ammann intended that the huge steel skeletons that constituted the towers should firstly be encased in concrete, then clad with granite. But the 1929 crash on Wall Street imposed unexpected financial restrictions. The result, while unusual for its time, has been praised for its aesthetic honesty. Ammann revolutionized suspension bridge design with his insistence that in long-span bridges the weight of the deck and cables was adequate for the task of stiffening and resisting strong winds, thereby eliminating the need for extra stiffening. The result was cheaper and lighter designs. He was also highly skilled at dealing with the complex politics and bureaucracy that surrounded the project. Ammann went on to put his ideas into practice on his last and longest span, the Verrazano Narrows Bridge completed in 1964.[7] In 1937 the Golden Gate Bridge, crossing the opening into San Francisco Bay from the Pacific Ocean, became, with a main span of 1,280 metres, the longest suspension bridge in the world until the completion of the Verrazano Narrows Bridge. Designed by Joseph Strauss, it was instantly acknowledged to be one of the world's most beautiful.

The Swiss engineer Robert Maillart took the aesthetics of reinforced concrete structures to new levels with his radical and sublime designs. Maillart approached reinforced concrete as a new material that demanded new aesthetic forms and structural understanding. This new kind of imagining produced designs of astonishing lightness both in construction and appearance, which had widespread influence throughout the twentieth century. He built forty-seven bridges between 1900 and 1940 and each has been acknowledged for its beauty and innovation. The Salginatobel Bridge of 1930 (see page 20), a hollow-box, three-hinged arch, is perhaps the most spectacular of his designs. While its span is not great, being only 90 metres, its location is dramatic, spanning as it does a sheer gorge in the Swiss Alps. Even the temporary timber formwork for the arch, designed by Richard Coray, has been widely declared a masterpiece. In 1947 the New York Museum of Modern Art held an exhibition of Maillart's work, the first such exhibition ever for a single engineer.

In his 1910 Le Veudre Bridge, with its 72.5-metre spans, the French engineer Eugene Freyssinet perfected the art of using not just reinforced concrete but of proto-prestressing – pre-tensing the steel reinforcement in order to counter concrete 'creep', the steady compaction that persists after the concrete has set. This was a phenomenon that Freyssinet discovered. Proto-prestressing allowed Freyssinet eventually to design the Plougastel Bridge in France. Completed in 1930, with three spans of around 180 metres, each one in itself greater than any previous concrete span, it was by far the world's largest reinforced concrete bridge. In 1946 Freyssinet completed the world's first major prestressed concrete bridge, the Luzancy Bridge in France. While its span of 55 metres was comparatively modest, its implications were enormous.

These spectacular constructions with their immense spans are usually celebrated as bravura displays by individual engineering giants. Often forgotten are the key craftspeople who pushed themselves beyond the limits of their art. As Henry Petroski points out, at the revolutionary Iron Bridge, the first major bridge to be constructed using iron as its main component, the responsibility for supplying the metallic parts 'fell to the local forge master Abraham Darby III, whose inherited and direct experience with cast iron was unsurpassed'.[8] Pioneering British engineer Thomas Telford began his working life as a stone mason and integrated this knowledge into his bridge designs.

Assigning credit to a single person for the design of these huge structures can also be fraught with politics and self-interest. In the case of Sydney Harbour Bridge, as far back as the opening in 1931 there were conflicting claims as to whom the ultimate credit should be given. In many ways the often heated dispute revealed the complexity of design and construction of a large modern bridge. It also was an expression of the fraught relationship in the 1930s between Britain and its former colony. Many in Australia were attempting to assert not just their formal independence, which had been achieved many years earlier, but also their separateness in terms of culture and identity. For some, the massive bridge was therefore a proud symbol of independence from the 'mother country', while for others it was an equally proud symbol of continuity and of belonging to the British Commonwealth and Empire.

The situation was deeply strained by the depression which hit Australia particularly hard during the years of the bridge's construction. Even the opening ceremony was an occasion of high drama as a monarchist army officer galloped in front of Australia's leftist prime minister, Jack Lang, and slashed the ribbon with his sword in the name of the king. The bridge was built by the British engineering firm of Dorman, Long & Company, but controversy existed as to whether it was designed by the Australian John Bradfield or the Englishman Ralph Freeman. The dispute, including correspondence between the two men, became so heated that the Institute of Civil Engineers said they would throw both out of the professional organization unless they calmed down. While Freeman apparently did the design computations, Bradfield seemed to have taken overall responsibility and thought up the type and shape of the structure. There were even strongly refuted accusations that Bradfield had simply copied the arch of the Hell Gate Bridge in New York. Most Australian sources claim Bradfield as principal designer while British sources generally insist it was

Freeman. As the Bridge approached its seventy-fifth anniversary in March 2007 the controversy flared anew, with confrontations over the true identity of the designer. Cooler heads point to the interwoven network of responsibilities that constitute any design team for a large modern bridge, even as far back as the 1930s.[9]

These long-span bridges were also both instrument and symptom of a revolution in the experience and imagination of space and time that swept through Europe and America from the middle of the nineteenth century. A quest for increased speed – of communication, transportation and daily interaction – was paramount.[10] Concerns, even obsessions, about regulation, reliability, interconnection and extended reach were corollaries of this quest. The most direct route possible was always chosen, subject of course to economic and social constraints, a route that cut directly across any physical obstacles that could cause delays or detours, and by such means that allowed the uncertainties of the weather to be pushed to one side. As Turner's famous 1844 painting, *Rain, Steam and Speed*, of a train of the Great Western railway rushing across Maidenhead Bridge signifies, the unique features of this revolution were steam and speed. These bridges were technologies of speed, often less about joining communities than about passing through and across them as quickly as possible.

Risk and the Culture of Span

A simple chronology of span, as presented above, belies a multitude of problems. Large span bridges, from their very inception, were integral to a culture of risk – structural, economic, social and aesthetic. Henry Petroski points to the numerous failures of early suspension bridges. It was, he writes, a 'sad chronicle', driven by overconfidence in 'analytical sophistication' rather than restraint in 'fear of the effects of scale'.[11] One of the earliest failures, the collapse of the Dee Bridge only a year after its completion in 1846, had enormous influence on designs that followed. Five people were killed and eighteen injured.[12] The Wheeling suspension bridge designed by Charles Ellet was an extraordinarily light and narrow structure. Its 308-metre span was the world's longest when completed in 1849. Then, in 1854, the deck was tossed about in a storm and the structure collapsed. Serious doubts began to be raised by engineers and the general public about the reliability of suspension bridges.[13] Urgent studies were conducted into the various instabilities affecting them, with distinctions being made between vibration and undulation, as well as debates about the virtues of various forms of stiffening, especially of the deck. The collapse of the Tay Bridge in 1879, a British truss and girder structure, showed that this was not a malaise confined to US suspension bridges. The failure of the huge cantilever Quebec Bridge in 1907 showed just how fraught the design of long-spans could be, no matter what type of bridge.

As late as 1888 it had been noted that over 250 failures of railway bridges had occurred in the USA and Canada in the previous decade. Many engineers at this time carefully studied these failures, trying to learn from mistakes. Nevertheless, as Petroski observes, by the close of the nineteenth century conspicuous successes in large bridge construction resulted in the engineering profession turning its attention away from its failures. It has been suggested that a structural pathology should be accepted as inevitable, rather than an unexpected aberration, and somehow be incorporated into the design. Perhaps the widespread hubris which co-exists with daring and vision could thereby be avoided.[14]

Science had enormous prestige immediately after the Second World War and the history of late-nineteenth century structures seemed irrelevant to most engineers. The scientific method, so called, ruled supreme and there was a search to find general theories of design.[15] However, problems still persisted and the collapse of the 854-metre Tacoma Narrows suspension bridge in 1940, shortly after its completion, forced a major rethink not just of computation but of the whole approach to studying design. While the dominant approaches stressed the use of handbooks, formula and emphasized mathematical analysis, innovative designers such as Robert Maillart also focused on visual form and physical behaviour, on evaluation and conception. He treated computation as merely an estimate, never as a truth. As Petroski suggests, 'virtually all design is conducted in a state of relative ignorance of the full behaviour of the system being designed'.[16] He uses the idea of the 'design climate', something that goes beyond mathematics and analysis to encompass cultural and social practices, values and attitudes, as well as the influence of individual personalities.

Attitude to risk is integral to any design climate. For many, concerns about risk and especially 'accidents' can touch 'deep fears about the shadow side of the successes of industrialization, scientific progress and technological innovation'.[17] Joost Van Loon, drawing on Heidegger's critique of technology, insists that risks offer opportunities to go beyond the constricting frame that is established by the extraordinary practical success of technology. He suggests that risks and 'failure', 'always have a split face' in that they can either be 'mobilized for greater systemic control and integration' or for 'radical change and innovation'.[18]

The West Gate Bridge Collapse

On 15 October 1970 I was working for the consulting engineers Freeman, Fox & Partners, helping to supervise construction of reinforced concrete bridges for the M5 motorway in England. Some of the construction workers called me over to where they were having a break in their normal place, sheltered from the weather under the bridge. I was told that there had been a terrible accident in Melbourne, Australia, with one of our bridges. They joked nervously about the safety of resting under the bridge. The underside of a bridge was, paradoxically, generally considered the safest place during construction, with the most danger posed by objects falling from the construction high overhead.

As a Royal Commission subsequently suggested, problems with the design (particularly of the stiffening sections) and the hasty construction timetable, were major factors in the collapse during construction of one of the world's longest box-girder bridges – and the deaths of 33 men. Approximately 2,000 tons of steel and concrete that had comprised the 112-metre span crashed onto the muddy bank of the Yarra River, bringing with it workers, equipment and sheds.

This construction was touted to be Melbourne's answer to the famous bridge of its arch-rival city, Sydney. Eyewitness accounts of these events are part of the telling of the bridge. A boilermaker's assistant who had been tightening bolts inside the huge box girder that comprised the superstructure of the West Gate Bridge recounts the moment when he was going for lunch:

> I was half-way down the scaffold . . . when the span I was standing in slowly started to sink down . . . I held onto the scaffold and it seemed like twelve seconds until the span crashed into the river. I don't know if I was knocked over inside the box, but after the span hit the bottom I was covered in mud, blood was running down from a cut on my head and I was standing up with a scaffolding tube across my neck. I saw a fire about 15–20 feet from me. I don't know what was on fire. All the

 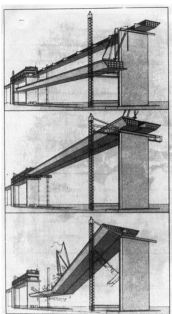

steel was twisted. A man I don't know was a short distance from me and was screaming for help four or five times and then I didn't hear any more. I could see the sky through a gap in the steel above me and about five minutes later some men came but they couldn't get me out until some time later.[19]

The Royal Commission found no fault with the materials, but the bridge Authority, the designers, the contractors and even the labour were all implicated to a greater or lesser degree. Economic imperatives and hubris, along with intercity rivalry, had probably pushed along both the design and construction at too rapid a pace.

Disaster on 15 October 1970 at West Gate Bridge, Melbourne, Australia, a photograph of the wreckage of the collapse from ground level.

A sketch of the collapse from the inquest files.

Super-spans and mega-cities: Hong Kong's Tsing Ma Bridge

While the contemporary reinvigoration and rebranding of established cities has often resulted in the construction of small, boutique, art installation-type bridges that are pedestrian-friendly, such as London's Millennium Bridge, the quest for the super-span has brought about new forms of urban conglomeration, new scales of urban assemblage, situations in which previous cities rather than just towns and villages are being stitched together into mega-cities.

Roebling was confident that suspension bridges of almost a mile span could be built one day.[20] His confidence was well-judged. By the close of the twentieth century several suspension bridges had approached and even exceeded one mile. San Francisco set the record in 1937, with a bridge of 1,280 metres. In 1964 New York's Verrazano Narrows Bridge set a new record of 1,298 metres. This was exceeded in 1981 by the Humber Bridge in England with a centre span of 1,410 metres. Then, in 1998, two bridges broke the one mile span – the Great Belt Bridge in Denmark with 1,624 metres and the Akashi Kaikyo Bridge in Japan with 1,991 metres. Even this span will be dwarfed if the bridge across the Strait of Messina, between the southern Italian mainland and the island of Sicily, is ever completed. After years of political wrangling and engineering speculation the project was cancelled by the Italian government in October 2006 amid concerns about costs, environment and the mafia exploiting the easy crossing to the mainland. The projected span of 3,300 metres was over two miles long. The towers alone for these super-spans are colossal. Those of the world's longest suspension bridge, the Akashi Kaikyo Bridge in Japan, are about 283 metres, while those for the cable-stayed Millau Viaduct in France, the world's tallest

bridge structure, are 343 metres. The Messina Bridge towers would have been almost 383 metres high if it had gone ahead. Only the tallest of buildings surpass this. In comparison, New York's Empire State Building is 381 metres to the roof, while Sears Tower in Chicago measures 442 metres and Taipei Tower 101, the world's tallest, measures over 449 metres.

In many cases these super-spans are merely one part of an immense project than can involve several huge bridges. Such is the case in Japan, one which involves two related super-projects linking the major islands of Honshu and Shikoku.[21] The Kobe Naruto Route is purely for automobiles and crosses between Honshu and Shikoku via the small island of Awaji. Beginning in the city of Kobe on Honshu the route heads east to the city of Naruto on Shikoku. Two broad stretches of water are traversed by two suspension bridges – the Ohnaruto Bridge, with a span of 876 metres, constructed between 1976 and 1985, and the Akashi Kaikyo Bridge, currently the world's

The Millennium Bridge, London, completed 2000, reopened 2002.

longest span at 1,991 metres, built between 1988 and 1998. During construction the Akashi Kaikyo Bridge had to survive a severe earthquake, while severe seismic and wind conditions imposed stringent demands on the structural stability of the Ohnaruto Bridge, issues that applied to the whole mega-project. Several kilometres to the south is another related super-project – the Onomichi–Imabari Route constructed between 1975 and 1999. This takes the road from the city of Onomichi on Honshu eastward to Imabari on Shikohu by joining seven small islands using ten bridges of different designs, several of huge dimensions. With a central span of 890 metres the Tatara Bridge became the world's longest cable-stayed bridge. The Kurushima Kaikyo Bridge is in reality made up of three suspension bridges joined together and covers over 4,000 metres. The ends of the northern and southern routes are linked by means of freeways, thereby creating a huge circular loop. With an older route, utilizing five suspension bridges, between Honshu and Shikoku already in place,

Akashi Kaikyo Bridge, Japan, constructed 1988–98.

the separation between two of Japan's major islands has effectively been broken down. Not only has transportation and communication been revolutionized, but established patterns and rhythms of daily life have been transformed, and there have been crucial shifts in cultures and identities. The density of major bridges in a relatively confined space is unparalleled.

Another example of a complex network of super-bridges is the project for the Pearl River Delta in southern China. While much of the current project is focused around Hong Kong with the giant Tsing Ma Bridge at its centre, the project will eventually encompass Macao,

A view of the proposed bridge over the Strait of Messina, Italy.

Tatara Bridge, Japan.

with a series of bridges traversing around 40 kilometres (25 miles) across the mouth of the Pearl River. This project is the very latest in a long history of cases where a super-bridge has been an integral technology for a process of assemblage that creates a modern city. Like the construction of Brooklyn Bridge over 100 years earlier, the Tsing Ma Bridge lies at the core of a cluster of super-bridges that gather disparate and fragmented urban and quasi-urban zones into a new cohesive entity.

Opened in 1997, the Tsing Ma Bridge remains the longest span that carries both road and rail traffic. It is integral to a series of new bridges that connect Lantau and other smaller islands to the Hong Kong mainland. While the prime purpose of these bridges was to allow the relocation of the international airport away from the crowded heartland of Hong Kong and onto the relative remoteness of Lantau Island, the constructions have also resulted in important shifts in Hong Kong's spacial identity.

The fragmented spaciality of Hong Kong, in particular the densely populated, crowded and seemingly chaotic heartland, has long occupied a pivotal place in the way Hong Kong has been

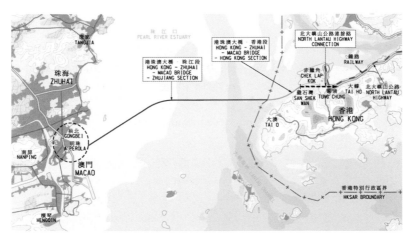

Map of Hong Kong – Zhuhai – Macao Bridge.

imagined and promoted, whether in film or tourism. Several new bridges have gathered the islands together creating a less fragmented sense of place, one that extends itself outwards via global communication corridors. These have also accentuated a spacial identity that is open, hyper-modern and orderly. The bridges, especially the Tsing Ma Bridge, have also become incorporated into Hong Kong's tourism promotion.

The Lantau Link, totalling 3.5 kilometres, opened in the middle of 1997, and was integral to connecting the new airport at Chek Lap Kok on Lantau Island with the Hong Kong mainland. The link is made up principally of the Tsing Ma suspension bridge and the cable- stayed Kap Shui Mun Bridge, completed in 1997, with a span of 430 metres. The Kap Shui Mun Bridge was, at the time of its completion, the longest cable-stayed bridge to carry both road and rail traffic. These bridges are connected by the 500-metre reinforced concrete Ma Wan Viaduct. Another cable-stayed structure, the Ting Kau Bridge with two spans of 448 metres and 475 metres, complet-

Brooklyn and Manhattan Bridges, New York, c. 1916.

ed in 1998, starts close to the mainland end of the Tsing Ma Bridge and connects the airport northwards to Hong Kong's New Territories. Yet another cable-stayed bridge, Stonecutters Bridge, is currently under construction about 5 kilometres from the three bridges that comprise the Lantau Link complex but which is an integral part of the transport network required by the new International airport. It is due for completion in 2008 and, with a span of 1,018 metres, this bridge will set a new record for cable-stayed bridges. The towers will be 293 metres, second only to those of the Akashi Kaikyo Bridge and the Millau Viaduct in France.

While the spanning capacity of suspension bridges remains unchallenged, there has been a sudden rise to prominence of long-span cable-stayed bridges as witnessed both in the Hong Kong and Japanese mega-projects, as well as in single structures such as the 1991 Dartford Crossing (or Queen Elizabeth II Bridge) over the Thames in England, and the Pont de Normandie in France, whose span of 856 metres is only slightly less than that of Japan's record-setting Tatara Bridge.

While some form of cable-staying has been used in bridge design for centuries, it is generally agreed that its modern incar-

The Lantau Link under construction, Hong Kong.

Cable spinning on Tsing Ma Bridge, Hong Kong.

nation, the cable-stayed bridge, began with the French engineers Poyet and Navier early in the nineteenth century. Once technical issues with stiffness and stability were overcome, cable-staying really took off after World War II, particularly in the rebuilding of Germany.[22] Cable-staying produces its own very unique kind of aesthetics, very different to that of suspension or box girder bridges. Its particular visual resonance has produced a mixed reception, despite designs of extraordinary beauty.

The Lantau Link has shifted Hong Kong's centre of gravity in numerous ways. Even in terms of land mass alone the change has been remarkable. Lantau island itself has tripled in size due to the reclamation of land required for the new airport, which was finally completed in 2000. But the bridges have effectively removed Lantau's remoteness, even its island-ness. The bridges of the Lantau link are integral to the new airport. This phenomenon is not unique to Hong Kong. The construction or development of international

Lifting of the last unit of the Tsing Ma Bridge, Hong Kong, March 1996.

Kap Shui Mun Bridge, Hong Kong, under construction.

airports, particularly within the penumbra of global cosmopolitan cities, requires massive logistical infrastructure, including rail and highways, along with their associated bridges. The Check Lap Kok airport is 34 kilometres from the old city centre. Ackbar Abbas suggests that 'it is not so much the airport being distanced from the city, as the city being integrated to the airport'.[23] The city and airport are fused into a single complex entity. Boundaries between the airport and the city are erased with infrastructure becoming the new interface. Hong Kong's local population stands at six million while the Check Lap Kok airport is designed to handle 38–45 million passengers a year and is a key revenue-generating facility. Abbas suggests that this disparity leads to people in transit replacing citizens, in number and perhaps in importance as well. The airport and the city are, from one perspective, part of the 'bridge', in the sense of the 'bridge' as an extended gathering, an extended corridor. Further influencing this shift in the centre of Hong Kong's gravity has been the opening of a Disneyland on Lantau island, which is also serviced by the Lantau Link.

Stonecutters Bridge under construction, Hong Kong.

There are other consequences of being integrated into a global economy. Frank Worsdale's novel, *Martyr's Bridge*, is post-September 11, post-Bali, fiction.[24] It describes Islamic terrorists from Afghanistan and South East Asia planning the destruction of the Tsing Ma Bridge as a spectacular centrepiece to a series of Far Eastern terror events. The attack on the bridge is described in terms of its critical importance for western society, its trade and business in the Far East, rather than in terms of Hong Kong or China.

All these bridges are dwarfed by the proposed Hong Kong–Zhuhai–Macao Bridge. With a projected overall length of about 35 kilometres it will shorten driving time from west of the Pearl River delta to Hong Kong by half an hour, creating a circle of city-suburbs within a three-hour drive. Large cities in western Guandong, such as Yangjiang and Zhanjiang, would also be included in this circle. This Pearl River Delta mega-city will cover 50,000 square kilometres and have a population of 40–50 million people. Interwoven with the system of physical transportation, of which bridges are crucial, are systems of optic fibre telecommunications.

Manuel Castells describes the Hong Kong, Shenzhen, Guangzhou, Zuhai, Macau–Pearl River Delta metropolitan system as an in-progress mega-city, a prototype of what is likely to become an increasingly common urban phenomenon. Mega-cities, suggests Castells, 'articulate the global economy, link up with the informational networks, and concentrate the world's power', but they are uniquely 'globally connected and locally disconnected, physically and socially'.[25]

A vision of flows and networks has been critiqued as being too neat. Mimi Sheller suggests a more messy analysis is required.[26] The underside of these super-bridges and mega-projects is likely to be found, not under the bridges themselves, but in the underside of global cities. The emphasis on establishing global connections can result in problems on a local level. As with previous forms of industrial and cosmopolitan cities, these mega-cities will attract vast numbers of digitally-poor people who are struggling to survive, who are trying to gain some advantage from just a proximity to global communication networks. Ackbar Abbas points to Hong Kong's long standing 'floating' identity, suggesting that until recently it has been a city of transients and a space of transit. He argues that Hong Kong will be increasingly at the intersection of diverse times and speeds. He raises questions about the nature of 'the local' under such circumstances, as a previously colonial city moves into becoming a global city.[27] Historic districts, shopping malls, food courts and theme parks have all been affected by the rapid rise of transportation infrastructure in global cities.[28]

The future of super-spans

While these mega-projects have plenty of supporters and admirers there are also doubters. Many of the projects have been poor performers – in terms of economy, environment and public support. There have been many examples of cost overruns and lower than predicted revenue.[29] Environmental groups and public protest forced the promoters of the Oresund and Great Belt links to take environmental issues seriously.[30] As has been seen, similar protests have had varying responses in the cases of the Golmud–Lhasa and the Alice Springs to Darwin railways. Certainly in the latter case there are serious concerns about its cost, under-usage and poor revenue generation. The Humber Bridge is a spectacular example with a 175 per cent construction cost overrun and only 25 per cent of predicted use.[31] In the cases of the Oresund and Great Belt links, there was a lack of trust by the general public, provoked by ongoing deception about key issues and an over-promotion of the benefits. While risk would seem to be an inevitable aspect of modernity, it has been suggested that there has been too much power and too much investment in these mega-projects, along with low accountability.[32] These are complex and hybrid projects that defy simplistic formulas for success. With such projects large cost blowouts are commonplace; it is difficult to predict why or what will cause them.

Are these mega-projects, with their super-bridges, merely the culmination of a modernist industrial fantasy, one that began over two centuries ago, a vision given specific final inflection by the technologies, the political, social, economic and cultural paradigms of the late twentieth century? Are they heading towards obsolescence in the era of virtual communications? Or, on the other hand, are they the precursors of a new order and scale of heavy engineering, one that further integrates local transportation and communication requirements, along with their territories, cultures and societies, into vast, highly regulated global networks within which the physical movement of people and goods is interwoven with digitalized flows of information?

The Protean Span

As has been seen throughout this book, the bridge is protean, multifaceted both in its form and in the responses it elicits. In addition, a fundamental question remains: what actually is a bridge? Obviously most bridges can be identified as such merely by their appearance. But there are more complex and deeper questions of meaning, purpose, function and imagination.

All bridges, from the few awesome super-bridges to the far more numerous small, simple, obscure and mundane ones, embody and express, constrain and develop a certain kind of world view. By necessity this includes a specific attitude or imagining towards social

life, political life, intra- and inter-community life, various forms of identity, power, the local–national–global nexus, aesthetics, the nature of science and technology, architecture and engineering, plus the relationship to the natural world. Bridges are always part of a complex ecology of ideas, of relationships and practices, of other 'technologies'. Bridges are always fundamental expressions of mythologizing, of fantasy-making. Sometimes this has been transparent and overt, particularly in the distant past, but in the modern world it is more usually something which is given a secondary status, seen as an activity of popular culture or art, a play around the core, fundamental techno-practical rationality of the structure. Throughout this book I have suggested that these myriad imaginative 'tellings' are not mere accretions or ornamentations, but utterly integral to the bridge and its bridge-ness.

A bridge at Höllentalklamm, Upper Bavaria, 1890s.

References

Introduction: The Telling of the Bridge

1 Alan Trachtenberg, *Brooklyn Bridge* (Chicago, 1979).
2 See Chale Nefus, *Bridges in Film*, http://www.historicbridgefoundation.com/ipages/film/1intro.html.
3 Jean Baudrillard, *The System of Objects* (London, 1996), p. 4.
4 Ibid.
5 Ibid.
6 Ivo Andrić, *The Bridge over the Drina* [1945] (London, 1994), p. 27.
7 See http://www.gen-eng.florence.it/starimost/ and especially http://www.gen-eng.florence.it/starimost/01_intro/hist_most/hist02.htm (accessed 20 February 2007).
8 Nefus, *Bridges in Film*.
9 For example Thornton Wilder, *The Bridge of San Luis Rey* (New York, 1939); Robert Waller, *The Bridges of Madison County* (London, 1993); Andric, *The Bridge over the Drina*.
10 http://www.singingbridges.net/about/index.html.
11 Iain Sinclair, *London Orbital: A Walk around the M25* (London, 2002), p. 109.
12 David Billington, *The Tower and the Bridge: The New Art of Structural Engineering* (New York, 1983), p. xiii.
13 Ibid., p. 3z.
14 Ibid., p. 4zz.
15 Ibid., p. xiv.
16 Ibid., p. 5.
17 Ibid., p. 24.
18 Ibid., p. 23.
19 Ibid., p. 37.
20 Ibid., p. xv.
21 William Wordsworth, 'Composed upon Westminster Bridge, Sept. 3, 1802', in *The Winchester Book of Verse*, ed. H. Lee (London, 1959), p. 133; William Wordsworth, *The Prelude* (New York, 1979).
22 Billington, *The Tower and the Bridge*, p. xv.

23 Ibid., p. 5.

24 Henry Petroski, *Design Paradigms: Case Histories of Error and Judgement in Engineering* (Cambridge, 1994), p. 7.

25 Ibid., p. 8.

26 Ibid., p. 10.

27 Ibid.

28 Philip Jodidio, *Santiago Calatrava* (Köln, 2003).

29 http://www.dartfordrivercrossing.co.uk/drc/hist3.htm and http://www.dartfordriver crossing.co.uk/drc/hist4.htm (accessed 20 February 2007).

30 Sinclair, *London Orbital*, p. 375.

31 Compare Trachtenberg, *Brooklyn Bridge*, p. 96 with the BBC documentary, *Seven Wonders of the Industrial World*, broadcast 11 July 2007 on ACT TV.

32 'Changing Our World: True Stories of Women Engineers, Extraordinary Women Engineers Project Coalition', *American Society of Civil Engineers*, http://www.asce.org/asce.cfm (accessed 23 May 2004).

33 Reyner Banham, *Los Angeles: The Architecture of the Four Ecologies*, (Harmondsworth, 1976), pp. 89–90.

34 Frank Worsdale, *Martyr's Bridge* (Singapore, 2004).

35 Jane Jacobs, *The Death and Life of Great American Cities* (New York, 1961); Aruna D'Souza and Tom McDonough, eds, *The Invisible Flaneuse?* (Manchester, 2006).

36 Ken Gelder and Jane Jacobs, 'Promiscuous Sacred Sites', *Australian Humanities Review*, (1979), http://www.lib.latrobe.edu.au/AHR/archive/Issue-June-1997/gelder.html (accessed 15 April 03).

37 Cynthia Cockburn, *Machinery of Dominance: Women, Men & Technical Know-How* (London, 1985); Marina Henderson, *Gustave Doré: Selected Engravings* (London, 1973).

38 Feodor Dostoevsky, *Crime and Punishment*, ed. George Gibian (New York, 1975); Wordsworth, 'Composed upon Westminster Bridge, Sept. 3, 1802'.

39 Andric, *The Bridge over the Drina*.

40 Justin Spring, *The Essential Edward Hopper* (New York, 1998).

41 Marc Augé, *Non-Places: Introduction to an Anthropology of Supermodernity* (London, 1995).

42 For example http://www.kurumi.com/roads/interchanges/gloss.html or http://www.weathergraphics.com/tim/dumbroad/design.htm or http://members.cox.net/mkpl/interchange/sdint.html (accessed 19 February 2007).

43 Banham, *Los Angeles*, pp. 89–90.

44 Gaston Bachelard, *The Poetics of Space* (Boston, 1970).

45 Paul Auster, ed., *The Random House Book of Twentieth-Century French Poetry* (New York, 1984), p. 13; Nafus, *Bridges in Films*.

46 Nafus, *Bridges in Films*.

47 Sandor Ferenczi, 'The Symbolism of the Bridge (1921)', *Further contributions to the theory and technique of psycho-analysis* (London, 1926), p. 353.

48 Ibid., p. 354.

49 Ibid.

50 T. S. Eliot, 'The Waste Land', *Four Quartets* (London, 1965).

51 Martin Heidegger, 'Building, Dwelling, Thinking', in *Poetry, Language, Thought* (New York, 1975), p. 153.

52 Heidegger, 'Building, Dwelling, Thinking', p. 152.

53 Georg Simmel, 'Bridge and Door', *Theory, Culture & Society*, XI/1 (1994), p. 5.

54 Ibid., p. 6.

55 Andre Spicer, 'Technical Questions: A Review of Key Works on the Question of Technology', *Ephemera: Critical Dialogues on Organization*, II/1 (2002), p. 65.

56 Ibid.

57 Ibid., p. 66.

58 Ibid.

59 Robert Romanyshyn, *Technology as Symptom and Dream* (London, 1989); on the relationship between technology, culture and nature, particularly in the influential works of Bruno Latour and Donna Haraway, see David Demeritt, 'The nature of metaphors in cultural geography and environmental history', *Progress in Human Geography*, XVIII/2 (1994), pp. 163–85; in terms of issues of temporality and mobility, that are critical for understanding bridges, see also Jon May and Nigel Thrift, eds, *TimeSpace: Geographies of Temporality* (London, 2001); Tim Cresswell, 'The Production of Mobilities', *New Formations*, 43 (2001), pp. 11–25; John Urry, *Sociology beyond Societies: Mobilities For the Twenty-first Century* (London, 2000).

60 Igor Koptoff, 'The Cultural Biography of things: commoditization as process', in *The Social Life of Things*, ed. Arjun Appadurai (Cambridge, 1988), pp. 64–94.

61 For an account of the 'true story' of the bridge over the river Kwai, certainly one with considerably more documentary veracity than the film, see: http://www.diggerhistory.info/pages-battles/ww2/kwai.htm (accessed 15 December 2006). It shows that bridge stories can be crucial in terms of struggles around memory; on the attempts at a contemporary rebranding of London's identity, see Joe Kerr and Andrew Gibson, eds, *London: From Punk to Blair* (London, 2003).

62 David Brown, *Bridges: Three Thousand Years of Defying Nature* (Buffalo, NY, 2005); Judith Dupre, *Bridges: A History of the World's Most Famous and Important Spans* (Köln, 1998); Bernhard Graff, *Bridges that Changed the World* (Munich, 2002).

63 Petroski, *Design Paradigms*, p. 3; Joost Van Loon, *Risk and Technology: Towards a Sociology of Virulence* (London, 2002); Paul Virilio, *Speed and Politics: An Essay on Dromology* (New York, 1986).

64 For example see Bridge Research: http://wwwtfhrc.gov/pubrds/summer95/p95su23.htm; http://www.krdotv.com/DisplayStory.asp?id=6405 (accessed 25 August 2004).

65 *The Dallas Morning News*, 28 February 1982.

66 Eyal Weizman, 'The Politics of Verticality: the West Bank as an Architectural Construction', in *Territories*, ed. Klaus Biesenbach (Berlin, 2003), pp. 65–118.

67 Eugene Levy, 1993, 'High Bridge, Low Bridge', *Places*, 8 (4), pp. 12–19.

68 http://www.italianhistorical.org/VerrazzanoBridgeStory.htm.
69 Eck, Diana, 'India's *Tirthas*: "Crossings" in Sacred Geography', *History of Religions*, XX/4 (1981), pp. 323–44.
70 Victor Turner, *The Ritual Process: Structure and Anti-Structure* (New York, 1977).
71 Iain Banks, *The Bridge* (London, 1992).
72 Thornton Wilder, *The Bridge of San Luis Rey* (New York, 1939).
73 Christopher Middleton, ed., *Friedrich Hölderlin and Eduard Moricke: Selected Poems* (Chicago, 1972).
74 Friedrich Nietzsche, *Thus Spoke Zarathustra* (Harmondsworth, 1978). This passage inspired the name of the art group *Die Brucke* in 1905.
75 For example http://members.aol.com/chopstcks/interest/bridges.htm; http://william-king.www.drexel.edu/top/bridge/orgs.html; http://www.brantacan.co.uk/bridges.htm; http://www.salvadori.org/kidbridges/bibliography.html; http://www.bridgesite.com;/ http://www.pbs.org/wgbh/nova/ bridge/resources.html; http://en.structurae.de;/ http://www.historicbridgefoundation.com/ipages/links/links.html (accessed 20 February 2007).
76 Susan Danley, 'Andrew Joseph Russell's The Great West Illustrated', in *The Railroad in American Art*, eds Susan Danly and Leo Marx (Cambridge, MA, 1988), pp. 93–110.
77 William Gibson, *Virtual Light* (London, 1996).
78 On the notion of 'thick description', see Clifford Geertz, *The Interpretation of Cultures* (New York, 1973).

1 Technologies of Extension: Burt Creek to Lhasa

1 See China Tibet Information Center: http://zt.tibet.cn/english/zt/040719_qztl/ 200402004726140729.htm (accessed 24 August 2005).
2 Scott Kirsch, 'The incredible shrinking world? Technology and the production of space', *Environment & Planning D: Society & Space*, XIII (1995), pp. 529–55.
3 Wolfgang Schivelbusch, *The Railway Journey* (New York, 1979).
4 Stephen Kern, *The Culture of Time and Space, 1880–1918* (London, 1983).
5 Kern, *The Culture of Time and Space*; Susan Danly and Leo Marx, *The Railroad in American Art* (Cambridge, MA, 1988); Theodore Waters, 'The Trans-Siberian Railway', *Frank Leslie's Popular Monthly* (1900): http://www.catskillarchive.com/ rrextra/stsib.Html (accessed 20 February 2005).
6 Stephen Daniels, *Fields of Vision* (Cambridge, 1993), p. 127.
7 Ibid., p. 126.
8 Ibid.
9 Ibid., pp. 124–38.
10 Charles Dickens, *Little Dorrit*; Herman Melville, cited in David Kynaston, *The City*

of London, pp. 149–50.

11 Christopher Chant, and John Moore, *The World's Railways: Early Pioneers* (Rochester, 2002), p. 21.

12 Leo Weinthal, 'The Cape to Cairo Railway and River Route', *The Empire Club of Canada Speeches* (1920): http://www.empireclubfoundation.com/details.asp?/SpeechesID=2562 (accessed 20 February 2005).

13 Chale Nafus, *Bridges in Films*, part 10: http://www.historicbridgefoundation.com/ipages/film/1intro.html (accessed 24 August 2005).

14 Judith Dupre, *Bridges: A History of the World's Most Famous and Important Spans* (Köln, 1998), p. 51.

15 See Dupre, *Bridges*, pp. 52–3.

16 Alan Trachtenberg, *Brooklyn Bridge* (Chicago, 1979), pp. 42–9, 59–60.

17 Susan Danly, 'Introduction', in *The Railroad in American Art*, eds. Susan Danly and Leo Marx (Cambridge, MA, 1988), pp. 1–50.

18 Danly, 'Introduction', *The Railroad in American Art*, p. 13.

19 Leo Marx, 'The Railroad-in-the-Landscape: An Iconological Reading of a Theme in American Art', in *The Railroad in American Art*, p. 204.

20 Daniels, *Fields of Vision*, p. 192.

21 Susan Danly, 'Andrew Joseph Russell's *The Great West Illustrated*', in *The Railroad in American Art*, p. 94.

22 Ibid., p. 93.

23 Daniels, *Fields of Vision*, p. 184.

24 Ibid., p. 193.

25 Nafus, *Bridges in Films*.

26 Ibid.

27 Anon., '"Sky Train" to Lhasa cracking and sinking, China not worried', *Tibetan Review*, XLI/9 (2006), pp. 4–10.

28 Tenzin Tsundue, 'The Train that cuts Tibet into two halves', *Tibetan Review*, XXXXI/8 (2006), pp. 32–3.

29 For example, compare the *Tibetan Review*, XXXX/9 (2005), p. 4, with *China Today*: http://www.chinapage.com/road/qinghai-tibet-railway.htm or with the *China Tibet Information Center*: http://zt.tibet.cn/english/zt/040719_qztl/moban.asp?id=03; http://zt.tibet.cn/english/zt/040719_qztl/moban.asp?id=08 (accessed 24 August 2005).

30 Pema Thinley, 'The Year China took Tibet to the abyss', *Tibetan Review*, XLII/1 (2007), p. 3. See also, 'Political repression intensifies as Tibet railway opens', *International Campaign for Tibet*, 30 June 2006: http://www.savetibet.org/news/newsitem.php?id=997 (accessed 20 November 2006).

31 Peter Bishop, *The Myth of Shangri-la* (London, 1989); Peter Bishop, 'Glimpsing Tibet: A Landscape of Closure & Loss', *Literature and History*, VI/2 (1997), pp. 56–72.

32 *The US-Tibet Committee*, 'railroad to ruin' (2002): http://www.ustibet.org/campaigns/railroad.html (accessed 23 August 2005).

33 *The US-Tibet Committee*, 'railroad to ruin'.

34 *Canada Tibet Committee*, 'Tibet Activists Target Bombardier's Annual Meeting', 7 June 2005: http://www.tibet.ca/en/publications/press20050607.shtml (accessed 23 August 2005); *Tibetan Review*, XXXX/9 (2005), p. 4.

35 For example, *Tibetan Review*, XXXX/1 (2005)), p. 3.

36 *Canada Tibet Committee*, 7 June 2005.

37 *Tibetan Review*, XXXX/9 (2005), p. 4.

38 Ibid., p. 4.

39 Singapore's Chinese Daily newspaper *Lianhe Zaobao* cited in ibid.

40 *China Tibet Information Center*: http://zt.tibet.cn/english/zt/040719_qztl/200402005661154649.htm (accessed 24 August 2005).

41 June Dreyer, 'Economic Development in Tibet under the People's Republic of China', *Journal of Contemporary China*, XII/36 (2003), pp. 424, 419; Gang Yue, 'Echoes from the Himalayas: the quest of Ma Lihua, a Chinese intellectual in Tibet', *Journal of Contemporary China*, 2004, XIII/38, pp. 69–88; Barry Sautman, 'Resolving the Tibet Question: problems and prospects', *Journal of Contemporary China*, XI/30 (2002), pp. 87, 88, 98, 101ff.

42 Peter Bishop, 'Reading the Potala', in *Sacred Spaces and Powerful Places in Tibetan Culture*, ed. T. Huber, (Dharamsala, 1999), pp. 376–85.

43 Sautman, 'Resolving the Tibet Question', p. 103.

44 *The US-Tibet Committee*, 'railroad to ruin'.

45 Dreyer, 'Economic Development in Tibet', p. 415.

46 Richard Howitt, Sue Jackson and Ian Bryson, *A Railway Through Our Country: Social and Cultural Impacts of the Alice Springs to Darwin Railway Project on Aboriginal people* (Sydney, 1998), p. 26.

47 'Working Together', *On Track: Australasia Railway Corporation Newsletter*, 7 January (2001), pp. 1–2.

48 See the Northern Land Council website: http://www.nlc.org.au/ (accessed 15 Octocer 2001); For a fuller discussion of the complexities around the project and its completion, see Peter Bishop, 'Gathering the Land: the Alice Springs to Darwin Rail Corridor', *Environment and Planning D: Society and Space*, XX (2002), pp. 295–317.

49 Howitt et al, *A Railway Through Our Country*, p. 101.

50 Ibid.

51 Ibid., p. 102.

52 Ibid., pp. 99–100.

53 Chris Gibson and Peter Dunbar-Hall, 'Nitmiluk: Place and Empowerment in Australian Aboriginal Popular Music', *Ethnomusicology*, XXXXVI/1 (2000), p. 39.

54 Howitt et al, *A Railway Through Our Country*, p. 145.

55 Ibid., p. 158.

56 Ibid., p. 165.

2 The Technology of Assemblage: Bridges and the Construction of the City

1 http://www.hiroshima-remembered.com/photos/hiroshima/index.html (accessed 2 August 2005).
2 James Patterson, *London Bridges* (London, 2005).
3 Aruna D'Souza and Tom McDonough, *The Invisible Flaneuse?* (Manchester, 2006); Michel de Certeau, *The Practice of Everyday Life* (Berkeley, CA, 1984); Nigel Thrift, 'Driving in the City', *Theory, Culture & Society*, XXI/4,5 (2004), pp. 41–59.
4 Deborah Stevenson, *Cities and Urban Cultures* (Maidenhead, 2003), p. 13.
5 Lewis Mumford, *The City in History* (London, 1966), p. 503.
6 Deborah Stevenson, *Cities and Urban Cultures*, pp. 17, 59; Nicholas Taylor, 'The Awful Sublimity of the Victorian City', in *The Victorian City: Images and Realities, Volume 2*, eds H. J. Dyos and Michael Wolff (London, 1973).
7 Raymond Williams, *The Country and the City* (London, 1985), p. 234.
8 William Wordsworth, 'Composed upon Westminster Bridge, Sept. 3, 1802', in *The Winchester Book of Verse*, ed. H. Lee (London, 1959), p. 133; Williams, *The Country and the City*, pp. 151, 159.
9 Feodor Dostoevsky, *Crime and Punishment*, ed. George Gibian (New York, 1975), pp. 51; 96–7.
10 Kirk Varnedoe, *Gustave Caillebotte* (New Haven, CT, 1987).
11 Taine cited in Grace Seiberling, *Monet in London* (Seattle, 1988), p. 40.
12 Seiberling, *Monet in London*.
13 Seiberling, *Monet in London*, p. 49.
14 E.D.H. Johnson, 'Victorian Artists and the Urban Milieu', in *The Victorian City: Images and Realities, Volume 2*, eds H. J. Dyos and Michael Wolff (London, 1973), pp. 458–9.
15 John Urry, *Sociology beyond Societies: Mobilities for the Twenty-first Century* (London, 2000), pp. 56–7.
16 Williams, *City and the Country*, p. 161.
17 Ibid., p. 162.
18 Edward Soja, *Postmetropolis: Critical Studies of Cities and Regions* (Oxford, 1995), p. 77. See also T. C. Barker, and Michael Robbins, eds, *A History of London Transport, Vol. 1* (London, 1975), pp. 300, 183.
19 Nafus, Chale, *Bridges in Films*: http://www.historicbridgefoundation.com/ipages/film/1intro.html.
20 H. V. Morton, *London* (London, 1944), pp. 49–51, 320–22.
21 Matthew Gandy, *Concrete and Clay: Reworking Nature in New York City* (Cambridge, MA, 2002), p. 123; Peter Rowe, *Making a Middle Landscape* (Cambridge, MA, 1991), p. 5.
22 Gandy, *Concrete and Clay*, p. 115.
23 Ibid., p. 14.
24 Dominic Ricciotti, 'City Railways/Modernist Visions', in *The Railroad in American*

Art, eds Susan Danly and Leo Marx (Cambridge, MA, 1988), pp. 134–6.

25 Gandy, *Concrete and Clay*, p. 117.

26 Ibid., p. 118.

27 Ibid., p. 119.

28 Ibid., p. 133.

29 Peter Rowe, *Making a Middle Landscape* (Cambridge, MA, 1991), p. 11.

30 Sigfried Giedion, cited in Gandy, *Concrete and Clay*, p. 123.

31 J. Tunnard and B. Pushkarov, *Man-Made: Chaos or Control?* Part 3 (London, 1974).

32 D. Bush, *The Streamlined Decade* (New York, 1975).

33 Rowe, *Making a Middle Landscape*, pp. 192–3.

34 Peter Merriman, '"A New look at the English landscape": Landscape Architecture, Movement and the Aesthetics of Motorways in Early Postwar Britain', *Cultural Geographies*, 13 (2006), pp. 78–105.

35 Gandy, *Concrete and Clay*, p. 15.

36 Sue Robertson, 'Visions of Urban Mobility: the Westway, London', *Cultural Geographies*, XIV/1 (2007), p. 74.

37 Justin Spring, *The Essential Edward Hopper* (New York, 1998).

38 Klaus Schroder, and Johann Winkler, *Oskar Kokoschka* (Munich, 1991).

39 Edmund Capon, *Jeffrey Smart Retrospective* (Sydney, 2000).

40 Michael Silk, '"*Bangsa Malaysia*": Global Sport, the City and the Mediated Refurbishment of Local Identities', *Media, Culture & Society*, 24 (2002), p. 776.

41 Ibid.

42 Ibid., p. 778.

43 Ibid., p. 779.

44 http://www.bridgeclimb.com.

45 David Billington, *The Tower and the Bridge: The New Art of Structural Engineering* (New York, 1983).

46 Philip Jodidio, *Santiago Calatrava* (Koln, 2003), p. 7.

47 Santiago Calatrava cited in Jodidio, *Santiago Calatrava*, p. 13.

48 Martha Arcila, *Bridges* (Barcelona, 2003).

49 Calatrava cited in Jodidio, *Santiago Calatrava*, p. 27.

50 Ibid.

51 Ibid., p. 23.

52 Ibid., p. 27.

53 Kenneth Powell, *New London Architecture* (London, 2001).

54 Sabine Gölz, 'Moscow for Flaneurs: Pedestrian Bridges, Europe Square, and Moskva-City', *Public Culture*, XVIII/3 (2006), p. 593.

55 Michael Hebbert, 'The Street as Locus of Collective Memory', *Environment and Planning D: Society and Space*, XXIII (2005), pp. 581–96.

56 Gölz, 'Moscow for Flaneurs', p. 593.

57 de Certeau, *The Practice of Everyday Life*; Brian Morris, 'What We Talk About When We Talk About "Walking in the City"', *Cultural Studies*, XVIII/5 (2004), pp.

675–97; Jon May, and Nigel Thrift, eds, *TimeSpace: Geographies of Temporality* (London, 2001).

3 Technologies of Connection

1 The *Guardian*, 28 April 2004, p. 12.
2 http://www.mexconnect.com/mex_/travel/dadams/da0303.html (accessed 13 August 2004).
3 See Marcel Mauss, *The Gift* (London, 1954); Jacques Derrida, *Given Time* (Chicago, 1992).
4 http://www.edmund-nuttall.co.uk/news/july2003/Bangladeshbridge.html (accessed 13 August 2004).
5 http://www.mekongexpress.com/laos/articles/dc_0694_laosaustralia.htm (accessed 13 August 2004).
6 Ibid.
7 http://www.mekongexpress.com/laos/articles/dc_0997_friendshipbridge3rd.htm (accessed 13 August 2004).
8 http://www.structurae.net/en/structures/data/s0000819/index.cfm; http://www.ibiblio.org/obl/docs/NN2003-03-24B.htm; http://viajar.clix.pt/com/noticias.php?id=1711&1g=en (accessed 13 August 2004).
9 http://www.aboitiz.com/corpnews.asp?id=20040713182445 (accessed 13 August 2004).
10 http://www.irrawaddy.org/news/2001/february-7.html (accessed 13 August 2004).
11 http://www.acdi-cida.gc.ca/CIDAWEB/webcountry.nsf/vLUDocEn/14DAEE678100; and http://news.bbc.co.uk/cbbcnews/hi/world/newsaid_1700000/1700492.stm; and http://afghanvoice.blogspot.com/2004/04/friendship-bridge-closed-uzbekistan.html (accessed 13 August 2004).
12 http://encyclopedia.thefreedictionary.com/Sino-Korea%20Friendship%20Bridge (accessed 13 August 2004).
13 http://www.tibetinfo.net/reports/outtib/border2.htm (accessed 13 August 2004).
14 Suha Ozkan, 'The Destruction of Stari Most', *Development Network*, 14 (1994), pp. 5–7, http://www.kakarigi.net/manu/azkan.htm (accessed 13 August 2004).
15 Ivo Andric, *The Bridge over the Drina* [1945] (London, 1994).
16 Ozkan, 'The Destruction of Stari Most'.
17 Judith Dupre, *Bridges: A History of the World's Most Famous and Important Spans* (Koln, 1998), pp. 24–5.
18 Nicholas Adams, 'Architecture as the Target', *Journal of the Society of Architectural Historians*, 52 (1993), pp. 389–90, http://www.kakarigi.net/manu/jsah-ed.htm (accessed 13 August 2004).
19 Ozkan, 'Destruction of Stari Most'.
20 Ibid.
21 see http://www.gen-eng.florence.it/starimost/ (accessed 20 February 2007).

22 Nicholas Adams, 'Architecture as the Target'.
23 Christine Evans, 'The Theatre of War, the Murder of Bridges', http://www.realtimearts.net/rt44/evans.html (accessed 14 April 2004).
24 Marcia Langton, 'How Aboriginal Religion Has Become an Administrable Subject', *Australian Humanities Review*, (1996), http://www.lib.latrobe.edu.au/AHR/archive/Issue-July-1996/langton.html (accessed 1 July 2004); also, http://www.austlii.edu.au/au/special/rsjproject/rsjlibrary/car/wtno8_may94/9.html (accessed 1 July 2004).
25 Ken Gelder and Jane Jacobs, 'Promiscuous Sacred Sites', *Australian Humanities Review*, (1979), http://www.lib.latrobe.edu.au/AHR/archive/Issue-June-1997/gelder.html (accessed 15 April 2003).
26 http://news.bbc.co.uk/2/hi/uk_news/wales/2681971.stm (accessed 28 January 2003).
27 Gavin Maxwell, *Ring of Bright Water* (London, 1960).
28 *West Highland Free Press* (*WHFP*), 15 June 1990, p. 9.
29 *WHFP*, 8 January 1988, p. 3.
30 *WHFP*, 21 January 1994, pp. 1–2.
31 *WHFP*, 8 September 1995, p. 1.
32 The *Guardian*, 15 July 1995, p. 6.
33 Lesley Riddoch, 'Over the turbulent sea to Skye', in *The New Statesman*, 8 August, 1997, pp. 36–7.
34 http://www.notolls.org.uk/skat/bridge.htm (accessed 24 February 2007).
35 Eyal Weizman, 'The Politics of Verticality: the West Bank as an Architectural Construction', in *Territories*, ed. Klaus Biesenbach (Berlin, 2003), pp. 65.
36 Ibid.
37 Ibid., p. 108.
38 Ibid., p. 111.
39 Eugene Levy, 'High Bridge, Low Bridge', *Places*, VIII/4 (1993), pp. 12–19.
40 Grady Clay, 'Ephemeral Places', *Design Quarterly*, 143 (1989), pp. 1–35.
41 Michael Gordon, *Reconciliation: A Journey* (Sydney, 2001), pp. 99ff.
42 Gordon, *Reconciliation*, p. 107.
43 See *Korcula Blog*, http://www.korculainfo.com/blog/index.php/category/peljesac/peljesac-bridge/ (accessed 25 February2007).

4 Spanning Technologies

1 Bent Flyvberg, Nils Bruzelius, Werner Rothengatter, *Megaprojects and Risk: An Anatomy of Ambition* (Cambridge, 2003), p. 1.
2 David Billington, *The Tower and the Bridge: The New Art of Structural Engineering* (New York, 1983), p. 249.
3 Cited in Flyvbjerg et al, *Megaprojects and Risk*, pp. 2–3.
4 Henry Petroski, *Design Paradigms* (Cambridge, 1994), p. 170.
5 Billington, *Tower and the Bridge*, pp. 54ff.

6 Cited in Bernhard Graff, *Bridges that Changed the World* (Munich, 2002), p. 73.
7 Jameson Doig, 'Politics and the Engineering Mind: O. H. Ammann and the Hidden Story of the George Washington Bridge', *Urban Affairs Annual Review*, 43 (1995), pp. 21–70; Henry Petroski, *Engineers of Dreams: Great Bridge Builders and the Spanning of America* (New York, 1995).
8 Petroski, *Design Paradigms*, pp. 8, 102–6.
9 Peter Lalor, *The Bridge* (Sydney, 2006).
10 Stephen Kern, *The Culture of Time and Space, 1880–1918* (London, 1983).
11 Petroski, *Design Paradigms*, p. 41; see also, 'Infamous Bridge Disasters': http://filebox.vt.edu/users/aschaeff/titlepage.html (accessed 13 February 2007).
12 Petroski, *Design Paradigms*, pp. 82ff.
13 Ibid., p. 125.
14 Ibid., pp. 97–9.
15 Billington, *Tower and the Bridge*, pp. 136, 213ff.
16 Petroski, *Design Paradigms*, pp. 93; 146–7.
17 Mark Ritter, 'Introduction', Ulrich Beck, *Risk Society* (London, 1993), p. 12.
18 Joost Van Loon, *Risk and Technological Culture* (London, 2002), p. 204.
19 See http://www.prov.vic.gov.au/exhibs/westgate/eyewitness.htm (accessed 12 February 2007).
20 Petroski, *Design Paradigms*, p. 136.
21 See Martha Arcila, *Bridges* (Barcelona, 2003).
22 David Brown, *Bridges: Three Thousand Years of Defying Nature* (Buffalo, NY, 2005), pp. 146ff; Petroski, *Design Paradigms*, pp. 172ff.
23 Ackbar Abbas, 'Building, Dwelling, Drifting: Migrancy and the Limits of Architecture. Building Hong Kong: From Migrancy to Disappearance', *Postcolonial Studies*, I/2 (1998), p. 196.
24 Frank Worsdale, *Martyr's Bridge* (Singapore, 2004).
25 Manuel Castells, *The Rise of the Network Society, Vol. 1* (Oxford, 1996), p. 404.
26 Mimi Sheller, 'Mobile Publics: Beyond the Network Perspective', *Environment and Planning D: Society & Space*, XXII (2004), pp. 39–52.
27 Ackbar Abbas, *Hong Kong: Culture and the Politics of Disappearance* (Minneapolis, 1997).
28 Eric Kit-wai Ma, 'Translocal spatiality', *International Journal of Cultural Studies*, V/2 (2002), pp. 131–52.
29 Flyvberg et al, *Megaprojects and Risk*, p. 3.
30 Ibid., p. 4.
31 Ibid., p. 42.
32 Ibid., p. 44.

Select Bibliography

Abbas, Ackbar, 'Building, Dwelling, Drifting: Migrancy and the Limits of Architecture. Building Hong Kong: From Migrancy to Disappearance', *Postcolonial Studies*, I/2 (1998), pp. 185–99
—, *Hong Kong: Culture and the Politics of Disappearance* (Minneapolis, IN, 1997)
Adams, Nicholas, 'Architecture as the Target', *Journal of the Society of Architectural Historians*, 52 (1993), pp. 389–90
Amin, Ash and Nigel Thrift, *Cities: Reimagining the Urban* (Cambridge, 2002)
Andrić, Ivo, *The Bridge over the Drina* [1945] (London, 1994)
Arcila, Martha, *Bridges* (Barcelona, 2003)
Auge, Marc, *Non-Places: Introduction to an Anthropology of Supermodernity* (London, 1995)
Auster, Paul, ed., *The Random House Book of Twentieth-Century French Poetry* (New York, 1984)
Bachelard, Gaston, *The Poetics of Space* (Boston, 1970)
Banham, Reyner, *Los Angeles: The Architecture of the Four Ecologies* (Harmondsworth, 1976)
Banks, Iain, *The Bridge* (London, 1992)
Barker, T. C. and Michael Robbins, eds, *A History of London Transport, Vol. 1* (London, 1975)
Baudrillard, Jean, *The System of Objects* (London, 1996)
BBC, *Seven Wonders of the Industrial World* (London, 2005)
Beck, Ulrich, *Risk Society* (London, 1993)
Billington, David, *The Tower and the Bridge: The New Art of Structural Engineering* (New York, 1983)
—, *Robert Maillart's Bridges: The Art of Engineering* (Princeton, NJ, 1979)
Bishop, Peter, *The Myth of Shangri-la* (London, 1989)
—, 'Glimpsing Tibet: A Landscape of Closure & Loss', *Literature and History*, VI/2 (1997), pp. 56–72
—, 'Reading the Potala', in *Sacred Spaces and Powerful Places in Tibetan Culture*, ed. T. Huber (Dharamsala, 1999), pp. 376–85
—, 'Letters to the Editor: Locals and Tourists Cross Over the Skye Bridge', *Studies in*

Travel Writing, V (2001), pp. 149–71

—, 'Gathering the Land: the Alice Springs to Darwin Rail Corridor', *Environment and Planning D: Society and Space*, XX (2002), pp. 295–317

Brewster, Anne, *Literary Formations: Postcolonialism, Nationalism, Globalism* (Melbourne, 1995)

Brown, David, *Bridges: Three Thousand Years of Defying Nature* (Buffalo, NY, 2005)

Bush, D., *The Streamlined Decade* (New York, 1975)

Capon, Edmund, *Jeffrey Smart Retrospective* (Sydney, 2000)

Castells, Manuel, *The Rise of the Network Society, Vol. 1* (Oxford, 1996)

de Certeau, Michel, *The Practice of Everyday Life* (Berkeley, CA, 1984)

Chant, Christopher and John Moore, *The World's Railways: Early Pioneers* (Rochester, 2002)

Clay, Grady, 'Ephemeral Places', *Design Quarterly*, 143 (1989), pp. 1–35

Cockburn, Cynthia, *Machinery of Dominance: Women, Men & Technical Know-How* (London, 1985)

Cresswell, Tim, 'The Production of Mobilities', *New Formations*, 43 (2001), pp. 11–25

Daniels, Stephen, *Fields of Vision* (Cambridge, 1993)

Danly, Susan and Leo Marx, eds, *The Railroad in American Art* (Cambridge, MA, 1988)

Davis, Mike, *City of Quartz: Excavating the Future in Los Angeles* (London, 1998)

Derrida, Jacques, *Given Time* (Chicago, IL, 1992)

Dickens, Charles, *Little Dorrit* (London, 1978)

Doig, Jameson, 'Politics and the Engineering Mind: O. H. Ammann and the Hidden Story of the George Washington Bridge,' *Urban Affairs Annual Review*, 43 (1995) pp. 21–70

Dostoevsky, Feodor, *Crime and Punishment*, ed. George Gibian (New York, 1975)

Dreyer, June, 'Economic Development in Tibet under the People's Republic of China', *Journal of Contemporary China*, XII/36 (2003), pp. 411–30

D'Souza, Aruna and Tom McDonough, *The Invisible Flaneuse?* (Manchester, 2006)

Dupre, Judith, *Bridges: A History of the World's Most Famous and Important spans* (Köln, 1998)

Eliot, T. S., 'The Waste Land', *Four Quartets* (London, 1965)

Eck, Diana, 'India's Tirthas: "Crossings" in Sacred Geography', *History of Religions*, XX/4 (1981), pp. 323–44

Evans, Christine, 'The Theatre of War, the Murder of Bridges', http://www.realtimearts.net/rt44/evans.html (14/04/2004)

Featherstone, Mike, 'Automobilities', *Theory, Culture & Society*, XXI/4,5 (2004), pp. 1–24

Ferenczi, Sandor, 'The Symbolism of the Bridge (1921)', in *Further Contributions to the Theory and Technique of Psycho-analysis* (London, 1926), pp. 352–6

Finch, Lynette and Chris McConville, *Gritty Cities: Images of the Urban* (Annandale, NSW, 1999)

Flyvbjerg, Bent, Bruzelius, Nils, and Werner Rothengatter, *Megaprojects and Risk: An*

Anatomy of Ambition (Cambridge, 2003)

Gandy, Matthew, *Concrete and Clay: Reworking Nature in New York City* (Cambridge, MA, 2002)

Geertz, Clifford, *The Interpretation of Cultures* (New York, 1973)

Gelder, Ken and Jane Jacobs, 'Promiscuous Sacred Sites', *Australian Humanities Review* (1979), http://www.lib.latrobe.edu.au/AHR/archive/Issue-June-1997/gelder.html (accessed 15 April 2003)

Gibson, Chris and Peter Dunbar-Hall, 'Nitmiluk: Place and Empowerment in Australian Aboriginal Popular Music', *Ethnomusicology*, XXXXVI/1 (2000), pp. 39–64

Gibson, William, *Virtual Light* (London, 1996)

Gölz, Sabine, 'Moscow for Flaneurs: Pedestrian Bridges, Europe Square, and Moskva-City', *Public Culture*, XVIII/3 (2006), pp. 573–605

Gottemoeller, Frederick, *Bridgescape: The Art of Designing Bridges* (New Jersey, 2004)

Graff, Bernhard, *Bridges that Changed the World* (Munich, 2002)

Hebbert, Michael, 'The Street as Locus of Collective Memory', *Environment and Planning D: Society and Space*, 23 (2005), pp. 581–96

Heidegger, Martin, 'Building, Dwelling, Thinking', in *Poetry, Language, Thought* (New York, 1975)

Henderson, Marina, *Gustave Doré: Selected Engravings* (London, 1973)

Howitt, Richard, Sue Jackson and Ian Bryson, *A Railway Through Our Country: Social and Cultural Impacts of the Alice Springs to Darwin Railway Project on Aboriginal People* (Sydney, 1998)

Jacobs, Jane, *The Death and Life of Great American Cities* (New York, 1961)

Johnson, E. D. H., 'Victorian Artists and the Urban Milieu', in *The Victorian City: Images and Realities, Volume 2*, eds H. J. Dyos and Michael Wolff (London, 1973), pp. 449–74

Jodidio, Philip, *Santiago Calatrava* (Köln, 2003)

Kern, Stephen, *The Culture of Time and Space, 1880–1918* (London, 1983)

Kerr, Joe and Andrew Gibson, eds, *London: From Punk to Blair* (London, 2003)

Kirsch, Scott, 'The Incredible Shrinking World? Technology and the Production of Space', *Environment & Planning D: Society & Space*, 13 (1995), pp. 529–55

Koptoff, Igor, 'The Cultural Biography of Things: Commoditization as Process', in *The Social Life of Things*, ed. Arjun Appadurai (Cambridge, 1988), pp. 64–94

Kynaston, David, *The City of London*, (London, 1995)

Lalor, Peter, *The Bridge* (Sydney, 2006)

Levy, Eugene, 'High Bridge, Low Bridge', *Places*, VIII/4 (1993), pp. 12–19

Van Loon, Joost, *Risk and Technological Culture: Towards a Sociology of Virulence* (London, 2002)

Lynch, Kevin, 'The Waste of Places', *Places*, VI/2 (1990), pp. 10–23

Ma, Eric Kit-wa, 'Translocal Spatiality', *International Journal of Cultural Studies*, V/2 (2002), pp. 131–52

Martin, G. H. and David Francis, 'The Camera's Eye', in *The Victorian City: Images and Realities, Volume 1*, eds H. J. Dyos and Michael Wolff (London, 1973), pp. 227–46

Marx, Leo, 'The Railroad-in-the-Landscape: An Iconological Reading of a Theme in American Art' in *The Railroad in American Art*, eds Susan Danly and Leo Marx (Cambridge, MA, 1988), pp. 183–208

Mauss, Marcel, *The Gift* (London, 1954)

May, Jon and Nigel Thrift, eds, *TimeSpace: Geographies of Temporality* (London, 2001)

Merriman, Peter, 'Driving Places: Marc Auge, Non-places, and the Geographies of England's M1 Motorway', *Theory, Culture & Society*, XXI/4,4 (2004), pp. 145–67

—, '"A New Look at the English Landscape": Landscape Architecture, Movement and the Aesthetics of Motorways in Early Postwar Britain', *Cultural Geographies*, 13 (2006), pp. 78–105

Middleton, Christopher, ed., *Friedrich Hölderlin and Eduard Möricke Selected Poems* (Chicago, 1972)

Morris, Brian, 'What We Talk About When We Talk About "walking in the city"', *Cultural Studies*, 18 (2004), pp. 675–97

Morton, H. V., *London* (London, 1944)

Mumford, Lewis, *The City in History* (London, 1966)

Nafus, Chale, *Bridges in Films*, http://www.historicbridgefoundation.com/ipages/film/ 1intro.html (accessed 24 August 2005)

Norberg-Schultz, Christian, *Genius Loci: Towards a Phenomenology of Architecture* (New York, 1979)

Ozkan, Suha, 'The Destruction of Stari Most', *Development Network*, 14 (1994), pp. 5–7, http://www.kakarigi.net/manu/azkan.htm (accessed 13 August 2004)

Patterson, James, *London Bridges* (London, 2005)

Petroski, Henry, *To Engineer is Human: The Role of Failure in Successful Design* (New York, 1985)

—, *Design Paradigms: Case Histories of Error and Judgement in Engineering* (Cambridge, 1994)

—, *Engineers of Dreams: Great Bridge Builders and the Spanning of America* (New York, 1995)

Powell, Kenneth, *New London Architecture* (London, 2001)

Reiter, Wellington, 'Bridges and Bridging: Infrastructure and the Arts', *Places*, IX/2 (1994), pp. 60–67

Ricciotti, Dominic, 'City Railways/Modernist Visions', in *The Railroad in American Art*, eds Susan Danly and Leo Marx (Cambridge, MA, 1988), pp. 127–46

Robertson, Sue, 'Visions of Urban Mobility: the Westway, London', *Cultural Geographies*, XIV/1 (2007), pp. 74–91

Romanyshyn, Robert, *Technology as Symptom and Dream* (London, 1989)

Rowe, Peter, *Making a Middle Landscape* (Cambridge, MA, 1991)

Sautman, Barry, 'Resolving the Tibet Question: Problems and Prospects', *Journal of Contemporary China*, XI/30 (2002), pp. 77–107

Schivelbusch, Wolfgang, *The Railway Journey* (New York, 1979)

Schroder, Klaus and Johann Winkler, *Oskar Kokoschka* (Munich, 1991)

Spring, Justin, *The Essential Edward Hopper* (New York, 1998)

Seiberling, Grace, *Monet in London* (Seattle, 1988)

Sheller, Mimi, 'Mobile Publics: Beyond the Network Perspective', *Environment &
Planning D: Society and Space*, 22 (2004), pp. 39–52

Silk, Michael, '"*Bangsa Malaysia*": Global Sport, the City and the Mediated Refurbishment of Local Identities', *Media, Culture & Society*, 24 (2002), pp. 775–94

Simmel, Georg, 'Bridge and Door', *Theory, Culture & Society*, XI/1 (1994), pp. 5–10

Simmons, Jack, 'The Power of the Railway', in *The Victorian City: Images and
Realities, Volume 1*, eds H. J. Dyos and Michael Wolff (London, 1973),
pp. 277–310

Sinclair, Iain, *London Orbital: A Walk around the M25* (London, 2002)

Smith, Denis, ed., *Civil Engineering Heritage in London and the Thames Valley*
(London, 2001)

Soja, Edward, *Postmetropolis: Critical Studies of Cities and Regions* (Oxford, 1995)

Spicer, Andre, 'Technical Questions: A Review of Key Works on the Question of
Technology', *Ephemera: Critical Dialogues on Organization*, II/1 (2002), pp. 64–83

Stevenson, Deborah, *Cities and Urban Cultures* (Maidenhead, 2003)

Taylor, Nicholas, 'The Awful Sublimity of the Victorian City', in *The Victorian City:
Images and Realities, Volume 2*, eds H. J. Dyos and Michael Wolff (London, 1973),
pp. 431–48

Thrift, Nigel, 'Driving in the City', *Theory, Culture & Society*, XXI/4,5 (2004),
pp. 41–59

Trachtenberg, Alan, *Brooklyn Bridge* (Chicago, IL, 1979)

Tunnard, J. and B. Pushkarov, *Man-Made: Chaos or Control?* (London, 1974)

Turner, Victor, *The Ritual Process: Structure and Anti-Structure* (New York, 1977)

Urry, John, *Sociology beyond Societies: Mobilities for the Twenty-first Century*
(London, 2000)

Van Loon, Joost, *Risk and Technology: Towards a Sociology of Virulence* (London,
2002)

Varnedoe, Kirk, *Gustave Caillebotte* (New Haven, CT, 1987)

Virilio, Paul, *Speed and Politics: An Essay on Dromology* (New York, 1986)

Waller, Robert, *The Bridges of Madison County* (London, 1993)

Weizman, Eyal, 'The Politics of Verticality: the West Bank as an Architectural
Construction', in *Territories*, ed. Klaus Biesenbach (Berlin, 2003), pp. 65–118

Wilder, Thornton, *The Bridge of San Luis Rey* (New York, 1939)

Williams, Raymond, *The Country and the City* (London, 1985)

Wordsworth, William, 'Composed upon Westminster Bridge, Sept. 3, 1802', in *The
Winchester Book of Verse*, ed. H. Lee (London, 1959), p. 133

Worsdale, Frank, *Martyr's Bridge* (Singapore, 2004)

Yue, Gang, 'Echoes from the Himalayas: The Quest of Ma Lihua, a Chinese Intellectual
in Tibet', *Journal of Contemporary China*, 2004, XIII/38, pp. 69–88

Acknowledgements

My main thanks must go to Sophie, Luke, Rafael and especially Louise, who have accompanied me on various bridge-hunting expeditions, helped with taking photos and generally supported the writing of this book, which took a little longer than I expected.

I would like to acknowledge support from the University of South Australia in the form of a Divisional Research Performance Fund grant. In addition, I want to thank all those people who have kindly chatted to me, generally enthusiastically, about bridges, shared their passion and pointed me in important directions. In particular I'd like to thank Andrei Gostin, whose freely-given technical expertise and time were most gratefully received. The last-minute suggestions by Vivian Constantinopolous at Reaktion were much appreciated. Some sections of the book have appeared previously in different forms in journals: 'The Soul of the Bridge' in *Sphinx 1: A Journal of Archetype and Culture* (1988); 'Gathering the Land: The Alice Springs to Darwin Rail Corridor' in *Environment and Planning D: Society and Space*, XX (2002), pp. 295–317; 'Letter to the Editor: Locals and Tourists Cross Over the Skye Bridge' in *Studies in Travel Writing*, 5 (2001), pp. 149–71.

Photographic Acknowledgements

The author and publishers wish to express their thanks to the below sources of illustrative material and/or permission to reproduce it:

Photo Pal Ahluwalia: p. 175; Australian Postal Corporation: p. 45 (this material has been reproduced with permission of the Australian Postal Corporation; the original work is held in the National Philatelic Collection); photos author: pp. 33 (top), 174, 204; photo William E. Barrett/Library of Congress, Washington, DC: 190; photos Brian Berger: pp. 58, 152; from *Camera Work*, no.3 (July 1903): p. 10; photos Heiko Dassow: p. 150; *Frank Leslie's Illustrated Newspaper*: pp. 28 (28 April 1883), 34 (29 January 1881); photo Gefyra SA Company: p. 186; photos Geoffrey Reed Communications: pp. 64, 101; photo Colin Gifford/Science & Society Picture Library: p. 119 (top left); photos Guildhall Library, City of London: pp. 31, 33, 38, 110, 111, 112 (top), 114 (top left), 115, 118 (top left); The Highways Department, Hong Kong Government: pp. 18, 30, 143, 207, 209, 210, 211; photos by kind permission of the Honshu-Shikoku Bridge Expressway Co., Ltd.: pp. 205, 206 (middle); photos Louise Hynes: p. 167; photos Sophia Hynes-Bishop: pp. 63, 99; photo Rafael Hynes-Bishop: p. 103; photos by kind permission of the International Campaign for Tibet (www.savetibet.org): pp. 65, 88, 92, 93, 94; Kimbell Art Museum, Fort Worth, Texas: p. 121; photos Lehigh University Digital Library: pp. 117, 193; photos courtesy the Library of Congress, Washington, DC: pp. 6, 9, 13, 15, 16, 17, 22 (top), 28, 32, 34, 36, 39, 42, 44 (foot), 47, 48, 49, 51, 53, 54, 75, 80, 81, 83, 84, 106, 108, 112 (middle), 114 (top right), 118 (top right), 127, 128, 134 (right), 136, 138, 160, 177, 208, 215; photos Jet Lowe/Library of Congress, Washington, DC: 44 (top), 82, 132; photos Adrien Mortini: pp. 26, 78, 116; Picture Library, Museum of London: pp. 33 (foot), 126; National Gallery, London: p. 74 (Turner bequest, 1856 - NG 538 - photo reproduced by courtesy of the Trustees, The National Gallery, London/© The National Gallery, London); photo National Railway Museum/Science & Society Picture Library: pp. 11, 194; The Newark Museum, New York State: p. 134 left (photo The Newark Museum/Art Resource, NY); photo Newspix: p. 178; photo Rex Features/Olycom SPA (683249A): p. 146; Saint Louis Art Museum: p. 124; photo Science Museum/Science & Society Picture Library: pp. 22 (middle), 109, 119 (top right), 183; reproduced courtesy of the artist (Jeffery Smart) and Parliament House Art Collection, Department of

Parliamentary Services, Canberra, ACT): p. 141; © State of Victoria, reproduced with permission: p. 202 (PROV, VPRS 24/P3 Inquest Deposition Files, unit 120); photo John Francis Strauss/Library of Congress, Washington, DC: p. 10; photo courtesy of Stretto di Messina S.p.A.: pp. 184, 206 (top); Toledo Museum of Art: p. 85 (purchased with funds from the Florence Scott Libbey Bequest in memory of her father, Maurice A. Scott, 1947.58 - photo Toledo Museum of Art); photos by kind permission, Wilkinson Eyre Architects: p. 148, photo J. Wayman Williams: p. 20.

Index